Sport
Ethnography

Sport
Ethnography

Robert R. Sands, PhD

HUMAN KINETICS

Library of Congress Cataloging-in-Publication Data

Sands, Robert R.
    Sport ethnography / Robert R. Sands.
        p. cm.
    Includes bibliographical references (p.) and index.
    ISBN 0-7360-3437-4
    1. Sports--Anthropological aspects. 2. Sports--Research--Methodology. I. Title.
    GV706.2 .S36 2002
    306.4'83--dc21   2001039232

ISBN: 0-7360-3437-4

Copyright © 2002 by Robert R. Sands

Acquisitions Editor: Linda Bump; **Developmental Editor:** Melissa Feld; **Assistant Editor:** Susan C. Hagan; **Copyeditor:** Bob Replinger; **Proofreader:** Jim Burns; **Indexer:** L. Pilar Wyman, Wyman Indexing; **Permission Manager:** Dalene Reeder; **Graphic Designer:** Fred Starbird; **Graphic Artist:** Yvonne Griffith; **Photo Managers:** Clark Brooks and Leslie A. Woodrum; **Cover Designer:** Jack W. Davis; **Photographer (cover):** © Christian Fletcher/SportsChrome USA; **Photographers (interior):** Loren Campbell (p. 30, bottom), Tom Roberts (p. 54), Linda Sands (pp. 30, top; 40; 68; and 74), Robert Sands (p. 37), Steve Sands (pp. xiii and xv), University of Illinois Sports Information Office (p. 132), Betty Volm (pp. 31, 38, 60, 104, and 115), and Belinda Wheaton (pp. 29 and 92); **Illustrator:** Alyce Taylor Cheska (frontispiece); **Printer:** United Graphics

Printed in the United States of America
10   9   8   7   6   5   4   3   2   1

Human Kinetics
Web site: www.humankinetics.com

United States: Human Kinetics
P.O. Box 5076
Champaign, IL 61825-5076
800-747-4457
e-mail: humank@hkusa.com

Canada: Human Kinetics
475 Devonshire Road Unit 100
Windsor, ON N8Y 2L5
800-465-7301 (in Canada only)
e-mail: orders@hkcanada.com

Europe: Human Kinetics
Units C2/C3 Wira Business Park
West Park Ring Road
Leeds LS16 6EB, United Kingdom
+44 (0) 113 278 1708
e-mail: hk@hkeurope.com

Australia: Human Kinetics
57A Price Avenue
Lower Mitcham, South Australia 5062
08 8277 1555
e-mail: liahka@senet.com.au

New Zealand: Human Kinetics
P.O. Box 105-231, Auckland Central
09-523-3462
e-mail: hkp@ihug.co.nz

To Alyce Taylor Cheska:

I can only build on the solid foundations of those who came before me. You, and the few sport and culture pioneers, built a mansion.

Contents

Foreword

In 1974 Edward Norbeck, Michael Salter, and I invited like-minded scholars focusing on the crosscultural study of play, games, and sport to form The Association for the Anthropological Study of Play (TAASP). The association held 13 annual conferences and produced 11 annual volumes, a newsletter, and a quarterly journal. Play as a broad multidisciplinary concept led to dropping the term *anthropological* from the association's name. The Association for the Study of Play (TASP) used many approaches of other disciplines but still reflected the use of anthropology. TASP's methods continue to bring a fresh perspective to sport and culture.

Key to TASP's perspective is ethnography, the signature method of traditional cultural anthropology, and it is used today in many academic fields. Ethnography also is popular in emerging fields, such as cultural studies, feminist studies, and ethnic studies. Books, collections, and journals describing and explaining methodology have been forthcoming, yet none offers the interested researcher a guide to doing good sport ethnography.

From the late 1800s throughout the 1900s sport researchers stressed the cross-cultural significance of sport. Some early scholars, such as England's Edward B. Tylor, the United States's Stewart Culin, and Germany's Von Karl Weule, used ethnography in gathering field data. In the latter half of the 20th century a new cadre of sport researchers produced studies using ethnography. Maria Allison and Gunther Luschen compared the structure of Navajo basketball and Anglo basketball sports systems, Kendall Blanchard studied the Mississippi Choctaw at play, Clifford Geertz investigated the deep play concept of gambling at the Balinese cockfight, Peter Nabokov authored a text on Indian running, Michael Salter examined play as a medium of cultural stability, and I looked at ethnic boundary maintenance in American Indian sports. But investigations were not limited to indigenous peoples. Gary Alan Fine spent time with a Minnesota Little League baseball team, using ethnography in long-term fieldwork to explore how play, games, and sport express cultural and ethnic identity.

Traditional approaches to the study of sport were brought to task in the late 1900s by a new generation of sport anthropologists, sociologists, psychologists, historians, and physical educators. Today postmodernism in the guise of interpreting cultural reality and the importance of the fieldworker's narrative in driving fieldwork have become extremely relevant. Gone is the distant, diffident, objective empiricism of the golden age of anthropology.

Robert Sands came to the University of Illinois at Urbana-Champaign in 1986 at the waning of the TAASP movement. Originally he started his doctoral work under my tutelage in the department of kinesiology (I also had a professorial appointment in the department of anthropology). After my retirement, Rob returned to anthropology to finish his PhD. His work with collegiate sprinters intensified his ethnographic approach and stressed the "participant" in participant observation as he balanced the oftentimes difficult roles of scientist/observer and athlete/population member. He was certain that this kind of ethnographic research could not only capture the cultural reality of athletes and coaches but also could be used to help make statements on the nature of human identity and behavior outside of sport. He has continued his investigative studies by working with junior college football players and surfers.

Much has happened since my retiring to paint Nova Scotia seascapes, but one constant in the exciting sport research climate is the importance of solid research tools. Ethnography remains an integral part of this enterprise whether we call it science, interpretation, or postmodernism. That is what marks Robert Sands's effort as important. His experience and training in anthropology, archaeology, ethnography, and sport make him an excellent conduit for describing, explaining, and illustrating the process of sport ethnography.

Alyce Taylor Cheska
Professor emeritus, kinesiology and anthropology
University of Illinois at Urbana-Champaign

Acknowledgments

This book had its genesis 14 years ago as I was mired in doing research on ethnographic methods for fieldwork I was doing on black and white collegiate basketball players. I read all I could on ethnographic methods. As I stepped onto the recreational basketball courts at Iowa State University, I found myself having to adapt the eccentricities of sport participation to what I was reading and learning. It was not so much that the tools of ethnography were different on the court than on a Pacific Rim island or in a highland Mayan community. I still interviewed players, observed behavior, took field notes, spent time writing up those field notes, and thought a lot about what my participation would contribute to the ethnography. Frequently, as I poured over texts and journal articles related to ethnography, I wished that there were accounts and treatises on ethnography written by those who had done sport ethnography and had gone through what I was going through at the time. I yearned for some familiarity with like-minded fieldworkers, with those who had spent time with coaches and athletes, had participated in games and practices, had become involved in the rituals that pervade sport and the athletic mystique, and had faced the risk of injury. Later, pursuing a doctorate in anthropology from the University of Illinois, I shifted only the sport, not the method, as I completed a participant observation of black collegiate sprinters. Since that first experience, I have explored different athletic cultures and venues—a track, a football field, and currently a surfbreak—from a perspective of the athlete and observer and have published on each of these studies. With each study, each culture of athletes, I find that besides the differences of what each sport selects for in behavior and requires in material items, equipment, and the like, the fieldwork has produced strikingly similar methods. Today, texts and journal articles on ethnography are numerous. The publications traverse disciplinary boundaries, and many involve authors who have no formal training in anthropology or even an understanding of the importance of ethnography. Yet not one speaks to those interested in doing sport ethnography. *Sport Ethnography* is the first.

In each of my studies, numerous athletes, coaches, and significant others gave of their time and energy to help with my fieldwork. Space does not permit even a partial list. My gratitude would fill volumes.

Along the way, I have received help and advice from many colleagues, but a few warrant special mention. I was a panelist on a discussion of ethnography in sport at the 1998 North American Association for the Study of Sport Sociology (NASSS) meetings in Las Vegas, and I then organized and was one of the presenters on a session on sport ethnography at the 1999 NASSS meetings in Cleveland. Of the five who presented their experiences in sport ethnography at that session, four were anthropologists. From these two sessions I would like to thank Anne Bolin, Jane Granskog, P. David Howe, and Larry de Garis for providing food for thought. I would also like to thank Michael Silk for his comments and Belinda Wheaton and John Baker for taking the time to read and make suggestions on the manuscript. I would like to extend my gratitude to Alyce Cheska, my mentor, colleague, and friend, for her advice and support over these 14 years. I would like to give special thanks to Linda Bump, a world-class editor who saw through the thousands of words I gave her and found a book—may her red pen never go dry. A final thanks goes to my wife, Linda, for her support through the always difficult period of writing.

Prologue

The ocean was alive, bringing clean four- to six-foot waves to Southern California beaches. This surfer's dream was courtesy of a hurricane spawned deep in the South Pacific. I was doing fieldwork on surf culture, and perfect summer conditions—a cloudless blue sky, a warm sun, and the waves—beckoned me. I wedged my 10-foot Yater board into the small front seat of my Miata convertible and threw in my summer rash guard and the ever-present Sex Wax. With the board hanging out like a sail, I roared out of my Ventura, California, driveway.

Just 10 minutes later I slowed from my dash and exited off the 101 North freeway onto old PCH 1—now a six-mile stretch of local beach breaks and intermittent RV parking. On pristine days like this, the breaks are crowded with all kinds—families and vacationers, young whiz kids (grommets), older surfers, or what I call soulsurfers, and more than a sprinkling of girls and

Attaching surfboards before leaving for my home break and daily fieldwork.

women. During the winter months, when the swell hammers the coast and the water temperature drops into the low 50s, only the devoted and obsessed venture out. I crept along at 45 miles per hour and passed Emma Wood State Park and the few transients who wander from beach to beach, park to park, rummaging in the same dumpsters day after day looking through new refuse and garbage left by visitors. One mile later, at the Solimar break, I saw the usual four middle-aged guys sitting in their lawn chairs on the side of the road overlooking the beach, studying the swell. They had beers cracked and straw hats covering their heads from the hot afternoon rays. Their bare backs and ample guts were bronzed the color of oak. Every day I passed these guys, and I knew that one of these days I was going to stop, introduce myself, and join another group of surfers.

I drove the length of Solimar, a collection of 20 houses hugging the beach, and came to Tanks and Mandos, surf breaks named after gas tanks and a grandmother, known intimately by those who spend lifetimes having them mark the boundaries of their sport places. To an ethnographer, or one who describes culture, the language of that culture is a code that when broken yields a vast amount of information. In surf culture, the labels of surfbreaks become important social markers, not only as locations on a map but also as keys to surfing tradition and history.

I learned these names not by consulting a map or surf book but by listening to surf "informants," those I spend time with while learning the culture of surfers. I learned about Mandos the month I picked up surfing. In *Surfer's Journal* (Allen 1998), I read about the grandmother who lived on the beach and surfed that break back in the 1950s. I also learned, several months later, from my wife's ex-husband—himself a surfaholic and a high-performance surfer—that the break was known as the Graveyard because the waves took so long to break that your life passed before you. It wasn't until much later that I finally found out why a break just south of Faria Beach was called Tanks. Twenty years ago, big petroleum tanks sat above the rock embankment and watched out over the surfers like sentinels. The tanks were eventually removed, but the place is still known as Tanks. The identity of the break is sustained by two generations and a third that never knew about the tanks.

After what seemed like forever but was really only a nine-minute ride down Rincon Parkway, one of the most scenic drives in Southern California, I reached Hobson's. For the short ride, the blue green Pacific was on my left, and to my right the coastal mountain range loomed a scant half mile from the beach. I knew I was almost to Hobson's when I passed the Wall, also known as Signals—the Wall for the concrete wall that separated day parking from RV overnight parking and Signals for the rail-road-signal standard that stood tall, across the road from the break. Thirty seconds later, I pulled into the small, tucked-off-the-road Hobson County State Park. I drove by the small concession stand and honked at Scott, a single father and grillmaster who lives in the trailer behind the stand. I claimed the last empty day-parking slot and thought that this must be my lucky day. I jumped out and quizzed the two surfers peeling off their wetsuits about the swell and conditions. Five minutes later—after hearing what I wanted to hear, "Clean, tide's going out, should pick up even more, there is a radical left and the right goes forever,"—I finished pulling on my summer wetsuit and waxing my Yater long board. I walked through the gravel campground, climbed over the stairs that arch over the rock embankment, and followed the steps to the beach 25 feet below. I paused at the top of the stairs and spent a couple of minutes surveying the small surf kingdom. I watched where the waves were breaking and how much time elapsed between swells. I walked out into the water, launched board and body over the first onrush of white water, and paddled out to the lineup to join three of my surf mentors and informants, Tom, Crazy Dave, and Gene.

Resting in the lineup, between waves and informants.

Before I sidled up to them, 100 yards from shore, and sat up and rested my hands on my thighs, legs dangling in the warm water, I knew what would happen in the next two hours or so. We will catch waves, wipe out on some, and catch rides on others for what would seem like minutes but last only 15 or 20 seconds. Between waves, they will talk and I will listen, absorbing what may seem to the casual observer like unrelated pieces of knowledge. After two years of surfing, I will more than occasionally chime in with my growing body of surf knowledge, proof that I am learning about surf culture and becoming part of it, a culture that chooses to ride waves as a form of recreation. Knowledge will flow naturally, passed between people as in any social situation. Instead of asking too many questions, I will let the events and contexts determine what I get out of the day's surf and interaction.

This day, conversation might revolve around Tom's teaching and surfing schedule and Crazy Dave's new 11-foot-long board, a true monster, or maybe touch on his wish to live in Hawaii and surf all day long. Conversation might include discussion of Gene's soon-to-be son-in-law, whom Gene is teaching how to surf, or we might talk about something we have never before touched on. I will catch one of many waves, maybe purl or nosedive and be chewed up by the wave. I will make my way back to the lineup, and Crazy Dave will laugh at me and tell me to get back on the board. At one point, the pod of dolphins that daily cruises up and down the coast will swim through the lineup. One or two may playfully catch a wave with us or explode out of the water in a graceful leap, and we will marvel at the communion of species on a wave.

I will absorb all this behavior, take part in it, and observe it. Three hours later we will pull ourselves out of the water and dry off. We will rinse our suits and boards off in the outdoor shower, tether the boards to our surf racks, and then stand around talking some more. Finally, we will get in our cars and make our way back to our homes. Even as I am driving, I am mentally going over the activities of the day and the surf lectures given by the wave-bound professors. That night I will sit at my computer and type in field notes. My feelings will somehow merge with the day's happenings. Later I will sit down and tell my wife of the day's events. Frequently, in the warm months, Linda will accompany me and go body boarding while I surf. We will sit at home later and talk of the people that populate those afternoons.

After two years, I find myself living the fieldwork, and I know that the hardest part of ethnography has passed. Most of the time spent doing ethnography is learning to walk through a foreign culture, just as a baby learns to take the first few steps. In taking the baby steps, the fieldworker travels through a series of developmental stages, or doors, learning more and more about the world around him. As each door reveals further knowledge, the fieldworker becomes dramatically more able to ferret out information not available before the opening of that door. I will spend time fertilizing contacts, learning the skills of the surf culture. The time spent ingratiating myself with the "natives" will ultimately flower into valuable data.

I finally paddled through the surfline, being rolled and caught inside the impact zone several times. Even though Hobson's had just about reached its critical mass of surfers, I knew where Crazy Dave and Gene would be, at the top of the point, waiting for the big sets to roll through, and that is where I found them. "Great day, isn't it?" I said as I paddled up beside them. *Great day to be working.*

Introduction

During my fieldwork, I developed several interesting hypotheses concerning surf culture and its juxtaposition with the culture that surrounds surfers. One hypothesis concerns the surfer's relationship between lexicon, or labels, and the environment. These speculations have sprouted from listening to surfers hour after hour, sitting on a surfboard or resting on beaches watching surfers, and then asking questions—questions that over time gently unravel the intricate web of relations that exist in the surfer's life. Another interest is the relationship between spirituality and the act of riding the wave. More than a few have likened this to a communion of a soul with the supernatural, not ghosts or gods, but with Mother Nature or Mother Ocean. Still another area of interest is the thread connecting ancient Polynesian and Hawaiian surfing with contemporary surfing, not only in the islands but everywhere there is surf. The spread of style, boards, and lifestyles from early 20th century Hawaii to the West Coast and Australia marked a process of cultural diffusion, which resulted in the retaining of some surf values and the hybridization of other values.

I could go on for quite a while with these hypotheses. There is much to learn about surfing, such as the rapid spread of surfing to females and families in the last 10 years, which marks a transition in surf generations. Older surfing fathers, and mothers, are now passing on surf knowledge to children, leading to gender equality that should affect participation in the next generation. The recent global surge of surf symbols in the guise of wetsuits, boards, surf posters, and surf videos and the capitalistic bent has created a visual and electric surfing style distinctly marked from the vast majority of "blue collar" surfers who daily frequent home and local breaks. There is even surf hooliganism and the protection of home breaks by local surf "Nazis," resulting in beatings and injury. The key to these areas of cultural research and others is the knowledge and experience gained through ethnography, specifically through participant observation.

Ethnography (in Latin, *ethno* for people, *graphy* for written) at its simplest is a tool for describing a culture in a qualitative sense. Previously the sole possession of anthropology, ethnography has now become the darling stepchild of many emerging academic social science fields as well as the traditional fields of sociology and political science. Demanding, labor intensive, soul giving, and long term, ethnography, especially participant observation, opens up vistas of cultures and groups inaccessible to other qualitative methodologies. Ethnography was once the rite of passage for novice anthropologists. Early ethnography was accomplished with foreign (at least foreign to the white, male, Eurocentric anthropologists) cultures. Surviving a year or two of fieldwork—complete with the culture shock, loneliness, and perils of living away from the familiar—meant that one had arrived as a professional anthropologist.

The process of ethnography, from initial hypothesis through planning, fieldwork, synthesis of data, and writing, represented several years of a person's life. Ethnography was not for everyone. Success did not come immediately, or even years down the road, to everyone who went through fieldwork. In an ironic twist, early ethnography always conjures up in my mind the mantra of the Marine Corps, "The few, the proud, the ethnographer."

Ethnography was birthed in a time when the wonders of the foreign and exotic were first being brought home to the enlightened and to the masses. Even before the early ethnographer stepped foot on an island paradise, a remote Mexican mountaintop, or the expansive African savanna, years of coursework and research was mandatory. In ethnography one learned by doing but only after learning what everyone else had done earlier. Ethnography has always been, and still is, a fluid and at times ad hoc exercise. There was nothing ad hoc to those 19th century pioneers concerned with the academic foundation for translating disparate cultural behavior into sweeping cross-cultural generalities that produced models or theories of human behavior.

Out of early work in anthropology grew the steps of ethnographic process: live with the natives, treat the stage of cultural behavior as a living laboratory, insert yourself into the web of social relations, and be accurate in your recording of data, in both observation and participation. Most important, retain at all costs the objectivity that the science of anthropology was built on. For such an enterprise, the teaching of ethnography lay in good hands. Those who did ethnography also taught it, and so in the generations since pioneers Franz Boas and Bronislaw Malinowski, ethnography has been handed down from one academic generation to the next.

The success of my initial fieldwork with college basketball players was as much a product of my being steeped in the tradition of ethnography and the holistic perspective and cross-cultural framework of anthropology as it was a process of hit and miss. I made mistakes and relearned methodologies, a process that all ethnographers have to go through at some point in their fieldwork to become "culturally fluent" in their experience. Now, even after experiencing fieldwork, writing books on sport and culture, and reflecting on my experience in college sprinting, football, and currently, surfing, I still have much to learn. I have played the culturally ignorant more times than I can count. I have asked questions about blocking in football that any football player should have known, about applying surf wax that any surfer should have known. I have yearned for a sense of objectivity while being labeled a "pussy" and a "fag" by football teammates for missing a block or pass. I have listened too many times to fellow athletes or acquaintances say the color of skin correlates with the length of tendons, calves, and penises. I sprinted through three years of the worst kind of pain known to sports, the last 20 meters of a 400, and I endured two seasons of a severely pulled groin, separated shoulders, and grossly misshapen jammed fingers to understand the culture of sport. Pain, risk, and danger translated into dislocated shoulders, concussions from runaway boards, and lacerations deep enough to demand stitches—symbols of rites of passage through stages of sporthood. These symbols were not so much emblems or medals of valor as they were proof positive that I had been there and had moved successfully to the next stage, the next skill level, and so on.

Today, academic disciplines blur. For many anthropologists, sociologists, historians, and even geographers, boundaries between disciplines are in danger of dissolving. New areas, such as cultural studies, feminism, literary criticism, and ethnic studies, straddle the study of Western society and the fast disappearing postcolonial, or postmodern, label of non-Western society. In their genesis is the creation of a more global enterprise that includes as its features of study hegemony, power, and neocolonialism. As these academic boundaries are reconfigured or lost all together, ethnography has been adopted, molded, and used by social scientists who are neither trained nor grounded in the traditional features of ethnography honored by anthropologists.

Sport Ethnography is not solely a field guide to doing ethnography in sport studies, nor is it only a collection of methodological case studies that illustrate field technique in specific sport situations, although some of each can be found in the following pages. Doing good ethnography is more than recording behavior through a video lens or microphone, catching behavior in a snapshot, or describing it in a notebook. Doing good sport ethnography demands more than just reading one of the many textbooks on ethnography and applying its concepts. Many texts in ethnography, and for that matter most anthropology texts, ignore sport as a viable means of studying human behavior (see chapter 1). Studying athletes who populate teams from Little League to the major leagues is now the domain of those not trained in anthropology or ethnography. By introducing ethnographic methods and elucidating fundamentals of fieldwork through examples of sport ethnographies done by anthropologists and others trained in fieldwork, this book provides the student or reader a familiarity not found in the sea of ethnography texts. I have found in my research that being athletic does not mean that one is an accomplished sprinter or football player; unique features and behaviors are essential to becoming a competitive sprinter or football player. The same holds true for an ethnographer. To do ethnography with athletes or a sport team, a familiarity with the ethnographic experience in sport is indeed helpful.

What I suggest in the following pages is that doing good ethnography requires at least a passing knowledge of areas that concern the quality of research, such as

- participant observation,
- culture shock,
- cultural relativism,
- establishing rapport,
- interviewing,
- an understanding of a contemporary definition of culture,
- interpretation of experience,
- analyzing and writing culture, and
- an understanding of ethics.

Good ethnography demands understanding of these areas if the fieldwork is to provide usable data or an experience that will lead the ethnographer out in the field again.

As much as ethnography has come to represent a field method in anthropology and now other social sciences, its importance is beginning to be translated outside the ivory tower. Business is beginning to use ethnography as a marketing and sales tool, and governmental agencies, such as the Census Bureau, use ethnography in their work. This book includes a chapter on the use of sport ethnography in these nontraditional areas. *Sport Ethnography* will also touch on recent controversy, in both anthropology and other social science fields, on the actual meaning of the data collected and the ultimate uses of such information.

Throughout this book, I will highlight important concepts with illustrations from my experiences in four field studies and from the experiences of others in the field—anthropologist and nonanthropologist alike—from triathloning to professional wrestling, from bodybuilding to weightlifting, from behind a TV camera to inside the dugout, from wrapping an ankle to wind surfing. This book, written by an anthropologist well versed in the use of the ethnographic method in sport, is a primer for those interested in doing good sport ethnography. No matter how well informed the fieldworker, each ethnographic experience will present situations and experiences that will test the ethnographer's ingenuity, creativity, and patience. Like the feeling one may have after completing a first marathon, a sense of accomplishment results from the completion of fieldwork. Fieldwork is indeed a rite of passage. I have also discovered that with each ethnographic experience I learn not only about a culture or group of people and the sport they play but also something more about myself. In that sense, fieldwork forces continuing self-discovery—and we all can use a little of that. Besides, I cannot imagine having more fun doing what I love as a job.

Overview

Chapter 1, "Sport Anthropology: Coming of Age on the Playing Fields," looks at the influence of early anthropology on modern ethnography and explores the history of the study of sport in anthropology and other social science fields. At the heart of any anthropological and ethnographic fieldwork is complete and long-term participant observation. The ethnographic text represents a cross-cultural perspective, useful in comparing with other cultures or groups. Most important, to any cultural researcher, generating human universals of behavior demands an emphasis on the similarities more than the differences.

Chapter 2, "Malinowski's Legacy," looks at perhaps the quintessential ethnographer of modern times, Bronislaw Malinowski. Many consider him the pioneer of the ethnographic method of participant observation. Malinowski and his many years of fieldwork provide an outline of salient features of method that will be covered in later chapters of the book. Today, over 30 years after publication and almost 60 years since his death, Malinowski's work still reverberates through ethnography.

The third chapter, "Into the Field," expounds on components of ethnographic research. This chapter introduces the nature of long-term ethnographic fieldwork by describing participant observation, the cultural "scene," the rapport between fieldworker and culture members, culture shock, and the investment of time.

Chapter 4, "Culture and Ethnography," deals with perhaps the most problematic theoretical issue of ethnography, defining the population one wishes to study. Traditionally, in ethnography, the maxim "One group, one culture" is applied to fieldwork done in distant, foreign lands. Yet with the world shrinking and political, economic, and indigenous identity (e.g., Native American, Australian Aborigine) emerging, culture has become a concept with many meanings.

In contemporary ethnography, such as sport fieldwork, the focus is not on the traditional grouping of culture, but on a group of people—athletes, for example—who during their interaction together make up a cohesive group. This collection of athletes shares intangibles and visible features, such as language, dress, even values of work ethic stressed by the sport involved. A cultural identity forms around the role of the athlete, defining who is and who is not a member of that culture. In other words, in sport there is grouping, or in an individual sport, a role or identity—for example, sprinter, gymnast, tennis player—that becomes the core identity. Included in this core identity are the secondary, more traditional features of race, gender, ethnicity, and so on. Thus one can study the culture of college football players in which culture refers to the group of players who share some or most of the behaviors and motivations that tie them together. Also included in this chapter is a discussion of the properties of culture: shared boundaries and behavior, cultural knowledge, and the representation of a cultural reality.

The next chapter, "Doing Ethnography," describes the tools of ethnography. Participant observation is an intensive and time-consuming way of acquiring data. The ethnographer can participate at a number of levels— from complete participation to a more passive shadowing of cultural members. In fact, at the conclusion of fieldwork, participation has included all those levels. The key to doing good ethnography is having the ability to turn the field experience into a meaningful text. Selecting the correct tools and using them in a way that produces clear, concise data makes the process of interpreting and writing ethnography much easier.

Chapter 6, "Analyzing and Writing Ethnography," represents the next step in the ethnographic process. The manner in which the culture and cultural reality is portrayed to the reader is integral to the formation of the text. The assumptions about what that cultural reality represents varies widely in contemporary culture. Today, several competing theoretical positions guide ethnographic research, and bitter controversy characterizes the use of ethnography in many social science fields. Implicit in this debate is the role of the ethnographer in the fieldwork process, or reflexivity—how much of the ethnographer is placed into the fieldwork equation. It will be clear that theory in ethnography, from a beginning in science and empiricism, has become a method used by many academic fields, each with an agenda for its use.

Chapter 7, "Risk and Ethnography," looks at the dangers of doing ethnography in today's world. When leaving the familiarity and comfort of one's own culture, entering the field can produce situations where innocence or ignorance can lead to risk. When considering sport ethnography, the ethnographer must be aware that physical injury is always possible. For the ethnographer, exposure to risks may validate in some way the reality of the experience. In many ways, this exposure to risk becomes a rite of passage for the ethnographer and legitimizes the experience to those being studied.

Chapter 8, "Ethical Ethnography," is concerned with the ethics and moralities of doing ethnography. Since the demise of colonialism, ethnographers have been held to task concerning their responsibility toward the people they study. Protecting their informants took on first priority in fieldwork and later publication, even over politics and patriotism. Codes of ethics and informed consents were created in many social science fields to acknowledge the moral responsibility of fieldworkers. In a modern world, where cultural knowledge is more than ever public knowledge, some ethnographers have resorted to using covert strategies in their fieldwork to offset the potential changed behavior of cultural members when informed of fieldwork. This chapter explores those issues as well as issues of sensitivity and the use of cultural knowledge in the academic world. The ethnographer today works in a world far different from the one of 80 years ago.

Chapter 9, "Experiential Ethnography," explores the nature of fieldwork when the ethnographer becomes the studied. Studying sport offers the ethnographer—if so inclined and sufficiently skilled to compete or perform with the athletes—an opportunity to become a participating member of the sport population. Implicit in this method is that the ethnographer journeys through a series of doors, or stages, much as athletes pass through the seasons in sport. Movement through a stage is celebrated as a rite of passage. The ethnographer's experience is not the central focus of the ethnography; instead, it validates the experience and behavior of many or most cultural members.

Ethnography has entered the third millennium, and chapter 10, "Ethnography for Hire," looks at ethnography as the newest trend in marketing and sales. Qualitative research in nonacademic areas differs markedly from research done in the traditional method. The ethnographer has an extremely short time in which to do fieldwork—a matter of weeks, even days—and the strategy is truncated and narrowly focused. The ethnographer loses control and objectivity because the research is geared to a specific area of inquiry and subsidized by a nonpartial party. Notwithstanding these restrictions, ethnography for hire has proven an effective and informational method for identifying and describing cultures of consumers. Ethnography for hire, and any ethnography for that matter, is necessary to personalize and humanize the bits of data that float in the abyss of the Internet. Humans still write those bits of culture.

The conclusion briefly discusses the direction of sport ethnography in the coming years as sport continues to be an important part of cultural and global interaction. To do good ethnography, one must be familiar with the method and role of an ethnographer.

Chapter 1

Sport Anthropology: Coming of Age on the Playing Fields

Using the field of anthropology of sport, the new emerging world order—where cultural contact between Western and emerging Third World cultures and reconstructed nations is, in major part, through sport—becomes more accessible to the human consciousness. Anthropology offers a formal and theoretical orientation to studying this reconstruction of world order, and the study of sport and culture becomes a necessity.

—Robert Sands, *Anthropology, Sport and Culture*

Anthropology is a very late addition to the social sciences. Dating back to the mid-1800s, the study of man was one way to assimilate all of the information coming back from explorations and the economic mining of unexplored lands, such as Africa, South America, the Pacific Rim and Australia. The first anthropologists attempted to build grand theories of cultural evolution using travelogues and anecdotal passages from missionaries, traders, and explorers. Much like today's anthropologists, 19th century anthropologists tended to study religion, kinship, economics, and political institutions. Primitive play and games were rarely written about. It has only been in the last 50 years that the study of sport and culture has taken root, and much of the work has been accomplished in academic fields other than anthropology.

This chapter will

- briefly explore the historical foundations of anthropology, and
- provide a look at the history of the study of sport and culture in social sciences.

In the Beginning: Ethnography

Anthropology came of age to Europeans and their American counterparts during the mid-1800s as unprecedented world travel, exploration, and economic and political domination over "primitive cultures" became a global phenomenon. In a way, anthropology was a result, not a cause, of what we know as colonialism. As far back as the 1500s, explorers were returning with stories of strange and exotic peoples and customs. Perhaps the most widely read narrative of all time is Marco Polo's accounts of his travels to and from China in the 13th century. Fueled by competition among European countries for riches and resources, travelers, explorers, traders, and missionaries wrote travelogues of discovery. Many were firsthand accounts of cultures seen for the first time. Motivated by religious beliefs or economic gain, these purveyors of the exotic and foreign offered up less than factual accounts of those "discovered." Ironically, the missionaries, in their zeal to convert these "heathens" to Christianity, may have provided the most authentic information on foreign lifeways. In the same breath, the men of the cloth portrayed the "natives" as savages, cruelly pandering to the sensationalism of these accounts back home. Still, by the time Darwin had dropped the bomb of evolution in mid-1859, travelogues only described but made no attempt to explain the strange—and to them bizarre—lifeways met by the traveler.

The theory of biological evolution had traveled a sometimes circuitous and extended journey across three centuries, detonating with tremendous impact on science and the Church. Yet it was only a decade later that two giants in early anthropology, E.B. Tylor and Herbert Spencer, formalized the evolution of culture. Tylor's work on religion was perhaps the most influential. He took the many travelogues and accounts he had read and, using the concept of culture, explained the many similarities discovered in his England and in pre-Christian religions. Facts, no longer curiosities, suddenly became related in a web of association defining humanity. Tylor's systematic sorting and construction of associations was probably the first example of a cross-cultural analysis, still the hallmark of anthropology. In 1871 Tylor published his *Primitive Culture* and used the concept of evolution, by then a centralizing focus in the natural sciences, as a framework in which to view the extreme variability found worldwide. Like his contemporaries, Herbert Spencer and Lewis Henry Morgan, Tylor could not shake the ethnocentric feeling that European males were the most advanced and that the "primitive" cultures were stalled in the evolutionary backwaters of cultural development. The ancestors of Europeans, and by proxy their descendants living abroad and colonizing the primitive cultures, had at some point passed through these stages on their way to the top of the evolutionary ladder. This ladder of evolution ran from simple to complex and became a synchronic look at cultural variety. This ladder was also arranged diachronically to illustrate the pace and changes of cultural evolution. Those most different from the Europeans in look and custom, the people of the Dark Continent of Africa, had to be the furthest from civilization. Indeed, Africans were thought of as subhuman, and colonial practices, even slavery, were rationalized as ways of pushing them up the ladder of human success.

These early anthropologists participated in fieldwork to supplement their theory of cultural evolution, but they relied most heavily on the mountain of quasi-ethnography supplied by the early intrepid amateur anthropologists. In many ways, these early evolutionists ended up rationalizing the spread of European colonialism. I characterize these early researchers as armchair anthropologists—attired in smoking jackets, puffing on pipes, sitting in front of crackling fires, and constructing grand theories of human development far removed from the cultural reality of the world. Their data were primarily pieces of anecdotal and even apocryphal information supplied to them. Anthropology today is far different in method and goals. Culture becomes the mechanism that makes people humans and not animals, and cultures become the behavioral adaptations to conditions of life.

In this book we will focus on sport as part of a universal behavior. All cultures in some ways participate in sport, and more important, sport has come to play an important role in determining and shaping this thing that anthropologists call culture. Not to give anything away, how we study culture and sport plays a major role in how we perceive its importance. If we relied on the method of Morgan, Tylor, and Spencer, only a fraction of the picture of the relationship between sport and culture would emerge. Instead of lounging by a fire or being supplied by random bits of information, the researcher becomes an intimate part of the people being looked at. This is ethnography—what this book is all about!

Anthropology Tackles Sport and Games

During the last half of the 19th century—the heyday of Eurocentrism—a fledgling look at sport and culture emerged. Initial studies focused on games. But even those looks were rare. The theorists of this period were more interested in looking at human behavior through economic systems, social structure, religious and political systems, marriage, and kinship than through such insignificant elements as sport and games. Most treated the subject as peripheral, of little interest to the study of human behavior.

According to Blanchard (1985), a more personal reason for this lack of interest was that most academicians came from the upper class—sport and games were enjoyed by the gentrified lower classes. Never being associated with such common behavior, these highbrows directed scant attention to sport, removed as it was from the mental aspects of culture. Indeed, the avoidance of studying sport as an expressive and ritual behavior was perhaps a product of a mental "colonialism," sport being too primitive to produce the right kind of cultural data.

A few studies during this period, however, bear mentioning. It is interesting that these first studies concentrated on games of physical and recreational activity—games were no doubt a more mentally challenging behavior. Tylor pursued the study of games and sport in an 1896 article on the similarities between Hindu pachisi and the Mexican game of patoli. Galvanizing to Tylor was the possibility that games such as these might offer clues about ancient cultural contact and aid in building theories of diffusion. At the turn of the century, ethnologist Stewart Culin, attached to the Smithsonian, produced a comprehensive and systematic study of the games and sport activities of 225 Native American tribes. Incredibly researched and highly theoretical in nature, Cullin's work advanced a view of Indian games and sport that fell along a four-category continuum and showed the importance of such activity in Native American culture.

Around the world and two decades later, Raymond Firth's (1931) study of the Tikopian dart match explored the inextricably connected relationship between competitive dart throwing, social organization, and the Tikopian belief system. Perhaps to portend the future, Firth suggested that further analysis of sport through ethnography was a fruitful channel of cross-cultural research. Possibly the best example of the study of sport and games in this initial period of research was Alexander Lesser's (1933) analysis of the Pawnee ghost hand dance. His research, a first-rate anthropological study, expressed the role of the game in Pawnee culture.

Research on Sport and Society Comes of Age

The 1960s ushered in a period of rapid social change in Western society, which was evidenced in how anthropology perceived non-Western society. The old-guard anthropologist—teethed on the classical works of Malinowski, Franz Boas, Margaret Mead, and A.R. Radcliffe-Brown, to name a few—were retiring and being replaced by anthropologists who were open to less-traditional academic arenas and pushing the boundaries of acceptable research. For the area of sport and culture, legitimacy was advanced by the seminal (1959) work of John Roberts, Malcom Arth, and

Robert Bush, "Games in Culture," that appeared in the major scholarly journal, *American Anthropologist.* This treatise, the first systematic attempt to define the concept of games cross-culturally, opened a debate among anthropologists concerning the place of sport in human society.

For the next two decades, through ethnographic investigations, the study of the effect of sport on cultural and social systems commanded notice in anthropology, as well as disciplines outside anthropology. In 1964 anthropologist Leslie White, in his presidential address to the American Anthropologist Association, suggested that a cross-cultural anthropology could provide an acceptable model for the study of sport, especially baseball, which White saw as a defining element of American culture. In an earlier study Robin Fox (1961) explored the use of magic in baseball by the Pueblo Indians in "Pueblo Baseball: A New Use for Old Witchcraft." Continuing the use of baseball in a cross-cultural perspective, former minor leaguer turned anthropologist George Gmelch revisited Malinowski's earlier work on Trobriand magic, comparing the belief system of the islanders with superstition in a 1972 article, "Baseball Magic." Pioneer sport and culture researchers Kendall Blanchard and Alyce Cheska carried out research on Native American sport and in their writings explored the role of sport in non-Western society.

Edward Norebeck was the most influential voice advancing the value of researching sport in a cultural context. In 1974 he, along with Alyce Cheska, Michael Salter, Blanchard, and others, formed *TAASP* (The Anthropological Association for the Study of Play), a cross-disciplinary group of scholars that included anthropologists, sociologists, psychologists, historians, physical educators, kinesiologists, and others. Yearly conferences were held through the 1980s, and annual proceedings were published. In 1985 Blanchard and Cheska published the first-ever cross-cultural study of sport, *Anthropology and Sport,* which was a successful first attempt at placing the study of sport in a rigorous methodology. Blanchard (1995) has since published a second edition. In 1999 I published a primer on sport and anthropology, *Sport and Culture: At Play in the Fields of Anthropology,* and a first-ever reader on sport and culture, *Anthropology, Sport and Culture.*

Without a doubt, during this two-decade renaissance of the study of sport and culture, the work that best fit sport into the scope of mainstream anthropology was Clifford Geertz's (1973) view of Balinese cockfighting, "Deep Play: Notes on the Balinese Cockfight." Treating the cockfight as a larger expression of Balinese culture, the work was more a part of the revolution in anthropology theory than a piece on the nature of sport in a cultural context.

If anthropologists were not involved in specific studies of sport over the years, at least some ethnographers were incorporating description of sport into their ethnographies. Fieldwork done on the Tarahumara of the Sierra Madres in northwest Mexico produced mention of their phenomenal, if not mystical, ability as long-distance runners. Studies on Native Americans also mentioned the integral part running played in Indian ritual and myth. With the proliferation of journals, magazines, *National Geographic* specials, and cable channels such as the Discovery Channel and the Learning Channel, not much of the world is left that has not been dissected, analyzed, and shown to readers and viewers. Sport is one of those cultural institutions that have been blanketed.

While anthropologists were barely warming up to the idea of sport as a viable expression of human behavior, other social science disciplines were embracing the study of sport as a means of expressing social systems. During the social upheavals of the 1960s and 1970s, social scientists looked at sport to help illustrate hegemony, racism, and social inequality played out on the very visible fields of American and international sport. During these two decades sport became a national barometer of success, and the Olympics became a platform for international social protest, starting with the 1964 Tokyo Summer Games and continuing with the riots in Mexico City and the Black Power Movement in the 1968 Mexico City Games, the massacre of Israeli athletes in the 1972 Munich Games, the 1980 Western-bloc boycott of the Moscow Games, and the 1984 Eastern-bloc boycott of the Los Angeles Games. While sport was becoming an important part of national pride or political rhetoric (illustrated by the institutionalizing of sport in Eastern-bloc countries), participation in sport at all age levels and in all social classes was on the rise. Sport became more than a means to an end.

Sport and Culture Research Today: The Failing of Anthropology

The decade of the 1990s has failed to promote the further study of sport in anthropology. Few anthropology departments offer undergraduate or graduate courses in sport and culture. Similarly, sessions on sport and culture are absent from major anthropology conferences. Outside anthropology, however, most social sciences offer a variety of courses on sport and culture, and some anthropology departments in larger universities cross-list courses in sport and culture with physical education or kinesiology departments. Even scholars doing work in sport and culture outside anthropology question why more attention has not been paid to such a global phenomenon: "What might explain the continuing marginality of sports to anthropology and social theory even as it is central to popular, folk and commodified life?" (Miller 1997, 115). Numerous academic works, both readers and texts, have been published on sport and society, and several academic journals cover sport studies, among them *Sociology of Sport Journal* and the *Journal of Sport and Social Issues.* Without the support of the discipline or the rank and file, anthropologists have produced some notable sport ethnographies in the last decade. Subjects include female track athletes in China (Brownell 1995), bodybuilding (Klein 1988, Bolin 1997), baseball (Klein 1991, 1997), black sprinters (Sands 1995), Kenyan distance running (Bale and Sang 1996), and junior-college football (Sands 1999e), to name a few.

Today, anthropology is one of the few social sciences that still find the study of sport beyond, or perhaps beneath, the discipline. I can posit a few reasons. Perhaps anthropology continues to hold on to the ideal that sport, or physical activity, is peripheral to the real study of human behavior, which is routed through religion, economic or political systems, or even language. Doing a kinship study is much more accepted than participating in and observing a Samoan wrestling match, and perhaps safer as well. Even in this age of participant observation, anthropologists may shy away from studying sport, teams, and athletes because many were not themselves athletes or because they found sport to be anti-intellectual. In my graduate years, all nine of them, I found just a handful of fellow anthropology graduate students who showed even a passing interest in sport. Finally, Western sport can be seen as colonial in nature, conservative and holding on to a hegemonic order. With a burgeoning interest in a postmodernism (see chapters 3 and 6), these 21st century academicians view Western sport, now a global phenomenon, as an agent that homogenizes identity and culture rather than celebrating diversity.

Elsewhere, I have argued that in light of anthropology's current search for its place in academia, sport offers a field of study that is becoming increasingly important in relations among cultures, nations, and societies. Indeed, to Peacock, anthropology with "humanistic interests . . . need[s] to probe the human experience in its variety, but also in its abiding unity. . . . We need not abandon the search for pattern and regularity in human life" (1996, 14).

Sport has been and will always be a significant element of cultural behavior, in our own backyard as well as in emerging Third World countries and long-standing tribal societies. Sport also reflects the enormous amount of cultural change through the impact of Westernization occurring in every corner of the globe. . . . In essence, sport has become both a barometer of social change and a leading

> agent of social change . . . it is also an extremely large window in which to peer into the tickings and cultural variation of human-kind. Anthropology seeks not the differences, but the similarities that lurk beneath the highly visible cultural expression that makes us all members of the human species. The study of sport is no different; sport reflects culture, and culture reflects sport. (Sands 1999b, 11)

Even as the few anthropologists and the larger number of nonanthropologists continue to probe the changing relationship of sport and culture, ethnography of sport provides a valuable perspective on cultural lifeways, beliefs, relations, and universals. It is through ethnographic research, including participant observation, that the statement "Sport reflects culture, and culture reflects sport" yields greater understanding. Anthropology, as a discipline, may never see its way to recognizing the value of research in sport and culture that other disciplines, such as sociology, psychology, and history, have acknowledged. Yet the anthropologist's unique research method and cross-cultural perspective can yield a rich and textured look at human behavior.

Chapter 2

Malinowski's Legacy

Proper conditions of ethnographic work . . . these consist mainly in cutting oneself off from the company of other white men, and remaining in as close contact with the natives as possible, which can only be achieved by camping right in their village.

—Bronislaw Malinowski, *Argonauts of the Western Pacific*

B ronislaw Malinowski is perhaps the first recognized ethnographer. He spent more than two years doing fieldwork in a foreign land and set forth the first scientific caveats of doing good ethnography. He believed it possible to conduct a scientific study of human behavior in the naturalistic surroundings of cultures, far from a laboratory. Set in the empiricism of the day, Malinowski's method strained to stay rigorous in application while bowing to the unpredictability of both the fieldworker and those being studied. Malinowski launched the modern ethnographic method, which soon became a staple method of an entire discipline, and later, the adopted method of many other disciplines. This chapter will explore the contributions of Malinowski and look at features that remain a legacy to his foresight as a cultural researcher:

- Participant observation
- Interpretation of culture through learning the language
- Malinowski's three ethnographic fieldstones
- Malinowski's diary and reflexivity
- Malinowski's legacy in contemporary ethnography

Going "Native"

A seafaring culture rich in magic and customs inhabits the Trobriand Islands, which lie off the eastern tip of New Guinea. It was to this chain of islands that Bronislaw Malinowski traveled at the outbreak of World War I. A London-trained Polish anthropologist, Malinowski had the misfortune (fortune to anthropology) to be traveling through the archipelago when war was declared. Halfway around the world, far from the trenches of France and Austria, Malinowski posed a problem to the British colonialists in Melanesia. His citizenship cast him as an alien, an enemy of the queen. The colonial administrators presented him with two options—return to Britain or Australia to be jailed and treated as a prisoner of war, or remain on the islands for the duration of the conflict. Malinowski chose the latter, as would most sensible people, and settled into an island existence, far from the madness of World War I. I am sure that most today would think that Malinowski had been dealt a perfect hand—"jailed" on a tropical island; in no danger of being gassed, shot to death, or maimed; and allowed to pursue his profession. The Trobriand Islands make Canada, the haven for draft dodgers during the Vietnam War, seem like Siberia.

Participant Observation

Malinowski participated in the Trobriand culture, living in a tent and later a thatched hut. From his morning and afternoon walks and discussions with the villagers to accompanying the islanders on their fishing expeditions, Malinowski was a Trobriand shadow. "He can take part in the natives' games, he can follow them on their visits and walks, sit down and listen and share in their conversations" (Malinowski 1984). He was left alone, for the most part, away from the distractions of other white men, and in the process became socially intimate with his island mates.

Malinowski was an outsider, an "other" to the villagers, while to Malinowski the islanders represented the "other." In this relationship of outsider to insider, bounded by familiarity and separated by differences, humans have expressed identity for thousands of years. Since our evolutionary journey reached the point where we joined others like us in groups and set those who lived apart as different, humans have always bonded with those sharing culture—the same customs, religion, even language, and perhaps the same skin color. Leví-Strauss, the famous French structuralist, labeled this a *binary opposition;* either we are "self" or we are "other." Malinowski walked a tightrope between objectivity and subjectivity, keeping the other at an objective distance from himself, but during the long years of forced residency becoming like the other. True to his calling, his classic *Argonauts of the Western Pacific* was a tome of description from a scientific distance.

Malinowski left his tropical "jail" and returned to England after the war, not as a prisoner but as a graduate student. He finished his dissertation and eventually became a professor. Besides writing up his fieldwork experiences—later to become a classic and influential series of monographs on economy and trade, kinship, family and sexuality, and farming and gardening—Malinowski also described a method of fieldwork that has become known as *participant observation*. Malinowski was not the first to engage in participant observation. At the turn of the century, Franz Boas was already involved in his groundbreaking research with the Kwakutl along the northwest coast of North America—Oregon, Washington, and British Columbia. Even earlier, Frank Cushing had spent considerable time with the Zuni Indians in the American Southwest. Malinowski's lasting contributions to ethnography were his formalization of the method as a process for writing ethnography and his shepherding of a generation of anthropologists through the pitfalls of fieldwork.

Interpretation

The key to unlocking the code of the Trobriand culture lay in Malinowski's efforts to learn the language. Most of culture is stored in the mind (see chapter 4 for further discussion on "mental" culture). Ethnography attempts to elicit that knowledge through active participation in everyday life and absorb enough of the lifeways to ask questions that will generate more knowledge, leading in turn to more questions. Ethnographers of the past, such as Boas—who had spent considerable time in the field combing through and collecting text—depended on translators to transpose not only the language but also the metalanguage of the culture, customs, rituals, law, and so forth. Malinowski's use of the language gave him free reign of the people and their physical space and opportunity to talk to them about what they were doing and saying.

Couched in the debate between postmodernism and positivism, a controversy rages today in anthropology and other social sciences about the process of interpretation by the fieldworker and the informants (people chosen by the ethnographer to be key contacts). In chapters 5 and 6 we will explore this topic further, but in brief, postmodernists would like you to believe that the current debate indicates that interpretation is a recent phenomenon. The fieldworker can never hope to understand fully the cultural reality of those being studied. The best the fieldworker can produce is an imperfect interpretation of what he or she observed, participated in, and later described. Interpretation has a much greater antiquity in anthropology, and Malinowski was the first to cross the pedestrian divide of understanding.

Malinowski's Fieldstones

In the introduction to *Argonauts of the Western Pacific,* Malinowski describes his method by concentrating on three principles, which I have termed *fieldstones,* of ethnography: (1) operate under good scientific aims; (2) live with the "natives"; and (3) use good data-gathering techniques. These three "stones" are still the backbone of modern ethnography. Recently, however, the first premise has stirred debate among anthropologists about whether such a people-oriented, human enterprise can be considered a science. Again we have to thank the lively debate between postmodernism and positivism for forcing us to consider whether anthropology and ethnography are similar to the empirical processes of the natural sciences and follow the same scientific steps: hypothesis, data gathering, testing, and theory construction. We will cover this topic later, but for now let us assume that ethnography is guided by a rationale that seeks knowledge to describe culture more accurately and eventually, through comparison, to formulate human universals of behavior.

Agreeing with the scientific foundation of the times, the staid and conservative Malinowski tried to suspend his personal judgment of the alien customs and rituals of the islanders. Malinowski was trying to be the perfect scientist and allow the data to speak for itself, unencumbered by the personal beliefs of his culture. Malinowski was attempting to use the principle forwarded by Boas, which we now label as *cultural relativism,* a doctrine of accountability in which human behavior is judged by the beliefs and mind-set of the population, not by the disapproving eye of the outsider. *Ethnocentrism,* in contrast, is judging those not of your culture based on certain values and premises you hold dear. Invariably, as we are all humans, those being judged tend to fall short of our behavior. Of course, this dichotomy is far too complicated to be defined by such simple opposites. We will tackle this topic when we deal with the thorny issue of comparability in ethnography. Today, any ethnographer will tell you that it is nearly impossible to stay detached and objective from those you are studying.

Obviously, the second and third fieldstones are now woven into the fabric of ethnography. Malinowski was a pioneer, suggesting that ethnography go beyond mere description through participation, listening, asking, and probing cultural meaning. Malinowski's data-gathering techniques included photography, mapping, charting kinship relationships, and interviewing the "natives." His questioning was open-ended, designed to obtain information that otherwise might have fallen through the cracks of prepared and controlled questions. Malinowski was often in the right place at the right time to observe and record cultural happenings that may have gone unnoticed had he not been present. At times, instead of waiting for a cultural event or oddity to occur, Malinowski would pose hypothetical questions that challenged the islanders to explore their own culture cognitively.

For over 40 years, Malinowski and his work with the Trobrianders was held up as the ideal against which to measure future ethnography. His writings were almost clinical, even sterile, in their objectivity and meticulous description of Trobriand culture. His theory of functionalism, although much out of date today, was an important school of thought that guided the research of countless future anthropologists and ethnographers. Based on the belief that anthropology could be a science, like physics or chemistry, Malinowski, E.E. Pritchard, A.R. Brown, and Margaret Mead wrote ethnographies that would become theories of human behavior. Each, I am sure, felt that as a scientist it was his or her job to formulate a hypothesis, visit a foreign culture, record observations, test the hypothesis using the data, and then construct a theory. In this equation, the ethnographer, much like the astronomer or physicist, became the silent or forgotten scientist. In science it was not the researcher that expressed the behavior—it was the variables given a certain situation. Malinowski was the epitome of scientific detachment, or so thought the anthropologists that followed Malinowski to their first and subsequent later field studies.

Unraveling of a Myth: Malinowski's Diary

On Malinowski's death in 1942, a colleague, Dr. Feliks Gross, helped his widow, Valetta, sort through his papers. Gross found a small, thick, black notebook that contained a diary handwritten in Polish that referred to Malinowski's fieldwork in New Guinea. His widow kept the book and after some random translations, put it away. She ended up taking many of Malinowski's papers, including the diary, with her to Mexico after the war. In 1949, when Malinowski's papers and collections from his office in London were sent to the widow Malinowski, she found two more notebooks labeled as diaries. She put them with the other work, and a decade passed before she, on a visit to New York, spoke of them to one of Bronislaw Malinowski's publishers. After receiving help in translation, she decided that the diaries should be published. In 1966 she published *A Diary in the Strict Sense of the Term* that exposed Malinowski—the man and scientist—and forever altered the role of the ethnographer in fieldwork.

In the diary that spanned two years of his fieldwork, Malinowski's personal feelings of his work, the islanders, and his family were starkly and explicitly laid out. Obviously, Malinowski never intended the diary to be made public. It contained emotional and vivid passages of a man alone, away from friends and family, missing his fiancée, frequently caught in a web of depression, and sickly from tropical diseases. Passages spill out Malinowski's feeling of superiority over the natives. Also chronicled is his frustration with what he perceived as the lack of the Trobriander intelligence. His diary also features fantasies about sex with old girlfriends and dalliances with local island women:

At 5 went to Kaulaka. A pretty, finely built girl walked ahead of me. I watched the muscles of her back, her figure, her legs and the beauty of her body so hidden to us whites, fascinated me. Probably even with my own wife I'll never have the opportunity to observe the play of back muscles for as long as with this little animal. At moments, I was sorry I was not a savage and could not possess this pretty girl. (Malinowski 1988)

Another passage describes Malinowski's frustration in his fieldwork: "As for the ethnology: I see the life of the natives as utterly devoid of interest and importance. Something as remote from me as the life of a dog" (Malinowski 1988).

Malinowski writes of the islanders as niggers (although there is some controversy on whether the Polish word used translates into "nigger"). In some passages he details their laziness and seemingly lethargic nature, and in others he talks of them as his friends. He writes vividly of his battles with tropical diseases and his exhaustion, and then places his fantasies on paper to read and reread at night. He vexes over the distance from his fiancée and spends a year of his diary arguing back and forth within himself on his feelings for her. In essence, Malinowski was bigoted, chauvinistic, depressive, and above all, lonely. Not to condone his writings or feelings, Malinowski's feelings were either a response to his isolation or a creation of his upbringing.

Valetta Malinowski poignantly supported her controversial decision to publish the diaries as a means to gather further understanding of a giant in anthropology and ethnography. "I feel," she wrote in the preface

that the psychological and emotional light shed by diaries, letters and autobiographies not only give one a fresh insight into the personality of the man who wrote certain books, developed a certain theory, or composed certain symphonies; but that through this knowledge of that man as he lived and felt, one is often brought into a closer contact and a greater comprehension of his work. (Malinowski 1988)

Besides revealing the hardships of fieldwork, the publication of Malinowski's diary forced anthropologists and ethnographers to contemplate the impartiality and detached objectivity of the fieldworker. In his foreword to the second printing of Malinowski's diary, noted anthropologist Raymond Firth wrote that

The relative lack of information about the personal reactions of the early anthropologists in the field tended to give an air of Olympian detachment to the published accounts. The anthropologist came, saw, recorded and retired to write up the material, apparently untouched by his or her experiences. . . . With publication of Malinowski's Diary, the stereotype was destroyed. Fieldworkers too turned out to be human—all too human. (Malinowski 1988)

In the space of one year, Malinowski went from myth to mortal, and anthropology went from empirical science to a crisis in identity. We will explore the current state of ethnographic theory in more detail in chapters 6 and 9, but a brief synopsis here will provide an understanding of what contemporary ethnography entails.

Contemporary Ethnography and Malinowski

In the 1960s an experiment in ethnography swept through the discipline. Instead of denying or submerging the role of ethnographer as it was played out in fieldwork—objective, distant, and detached—ethnography began incorporating the fieldworker into the process. As Clifford Geertz, one of the pioneers of contemporary ethnography has said, the ethnographer must attempt a difficult feat—becoming an insider while simultaneously maintaining an analytical distance to process cultural information. In seminal work on Balinese cockfights, Geertz was one of the first to suggest that the ethnographer was negotiating with informants and that the ethnography was a somewhat fictional text. If this was the case, then the fieldworker became part of the process of ethnography. This circumstance has become known as *reflexivity,* or how the ethnographer's cultural background affects the ethnography. Still, ethnography was thought to be an enterprise in which the ethnographer, through rapport with informants and his or her own participation, was able to understand the cultural perspective of the informants' culture. The description was composed of social data, values, and institutions, and was expressed in part through material items of the culture. It was the nature of this data and the cultural members that precluded the use of an empirical science. At the same time, ethnography and its participant observation was the only method through which such human "facts" could be elicited. Admittedly, ethnography went from being a tool in an empirical science to an imperfect yet usable tool for a humanistic science. From being a silent partner, the ethnographer now has become part of the story. Writes Dennison Nash, "No longer is the cultural researcher/ ethnographer considered to be some kind of super hero cross-cultural reporting machine. . . . They are affected by the same kinds of forces that shape their subjects" (Nash 1999, 11).

There is yet another look at ethnography and the application of its method to understanding the world around us. It was spawned out of postmodern thought that has swept through the humanities and sciences in the last two decades. Not to become bogged down in its intricacies, postmodernism looks at the changing world in response to a reconfiguring of what used to be the traditional colonial (European) and American (before and during the Vietnam War) world order. With the demise of colonialism and the end of the Vietnam War, a radical shift, and sometimes birth, of national and cultural identities has occurred. Recently, postmodernism has become identified with more than just globalization and postcolonialism. Although the roots of that enterprise were birthed in the radically shifting cultural and national boundaries of the middle 20th century, contemporary postmodernism is now linked to distinct and unique methodology and experimental and often radical perspectives of field data and the use of such data. The early classical ethnography, described in the introduction, was either done for the colonial administrators or used by them to understand the peoples and cultures being administered to.

Although colonialism has ended, postmodernists still feel that ethnographers—who believe a science is possible in cultural research—continue to operate, consciously or unconsciously, under a colonial mindset when doing fieldwork. Moreover, the traditional perspective of one culture, one people no longer applies in a fragmentary and constantly shifting global and national social-cultural landscape. To some extreme postmodernists, the ethnographer must remain an outsider, and the traditional ethnographic method no longer works. What the ethnographer then produces is subjective and negotiated—a fictional account that cannot reproduce the cultural reality of those being studied. Such accounts lack any kind of scientific or explanatory power. To some, like George Marcus and James Clifford, the accounts are a humanistic literary device that is, at best, a text of the details or the ethnographer's autobiographical journey through experience.

Works in ethnography since the 1980s differ from the traditional or classic monographs in several ways, all relating to the changes in global order and an increasingly connected world. First, the perception of monolithic identity of individual cultures has been replaced by treating the local culture as being embedded in a larger regional and world nexus. Second, much of recent ethnography is focused on a topic of interest. The goal of presenting a holistic picture of a culture seems to be no longer viable—no one can cover all the complex and complicated angles of a people. In the case of sport ethnography, it is possible to conceive of an athletic team or group, even athletes of a sport, as a culture. In this instance the notion of one people, one culture can still apply in a modernistic sort of way. Much of sport ethnography today reflects a third trend in ethnography—doing fieldwork in Western industrialized cultures. Although much of this research might superficially resemble a sociological study, the different perspective and fieldwork methodology of ethnography allow a variety of traditional and emerging fields of study to provide a more richly detailed look at human behavior.

As you might already have noticed, my take on this debate follows the traditional and still majority view that ethnography can be a formalized, systematic tool for explaining cultural differences and similarities—so much for the impartiality of the describer. As indicated, we will revisit this debate later in the book (see chapters 6 and 9). Even with this raging debate, however, one would be hard pressed to find ethnographers who have not consciously or unconsciously walked in Malinowski's footsteps on their way to completing their fieldwork. As we explore the ethnographic process and its application in sport studies, this legacy will percolate to the surface. Malinowski may have been cut down to being mortal by his diary. Yet his legacy and perseverance remain indelibly etched in the ethnographic process.

Chapter 3

Into the Field

He can take part in the natives' games, he can follow them on their visits and walks, sit down and listen and share in their conversations.

—Bronislaw Malinowski, *Argonauts of the Western Pacific*

It is perhaps odd, but not too surprising, that I looked beyond academia for inspiration to engage in sport ethnography. Even before I was wrestling with combining anthropology and sport while working on my MA, even before I was exposing myself to all fields of anthropology as an undergraduate, even before I had decided when I was a high school sophomore that I wanted to be a college professor, I had decided that a good way to find out about what really made athletes tick and sport so popular was to play the sport. At age 12—in the summer of 1969, when American society was being ripped asunder by the Vietnam War, demonstrations, race riots, and the Peace Movement—I read George Plimpton's *Paper Lion*, a recounting of the month Plimpton spent in the summer training camp of the Detroit Lions. I was fascinated by Plimpton's ability to flesh out the one-dimensional Detroit Lions. The private lives of athletes were then hardly the grist for the mill that they are today. I was attracted to the Walter Mitty fantasy world engineered by Plimpton in his sojourn with the Lions. Almost every 12-year-old boy, whether an athlete or not, daydreams about heroic performances on the playing fields, and here was this 30-something Harvard-trained journalist playing quarterback with the Detroit Lions, for God's sakes. "I was going there as the Lions' last-string quarterback to join the team as an amateur to undergo first hand the life of the professional, and, hopefully, to describe the experience in a book" (Plimpton 1989, 2). His excursion into professional football suggested to a daydreaming adolescent that if Plimpton could do it, why couldn't he? Now when I look back on that summer, I realize that I had already started on the road to becoming an ethnographer—I just didn't know that's what it was. Plimpton would be the first to agree that his tale was far from an ethnography, falling short on research design, formal analysis, and extended period of research, to name a few. Yet I need only mention his name when others wonder what I do, and I become today's George Plimpton.

In an earlier book about his experience playing in a postseason game with baseball's major-league all-stars in Yankee Stadium—Plimpton always started at the top—he wrote experiences that were about "someone with the temerity to climb the field-box railings to try the sport oneself, just to see how one got along. . . . to play out the fantasies, the daydreams that so many people have . . . [like] ripping through the Green Bay secondary" (1969, 2). Plimpton lived to write about his one-month "tryout" with the Lions during their summer camp and went on to do similar books on boxing, hockey, and golf.

Perhaps Plimpton could be characterized as a closet ethnographer. Certainly his participation and observation, although less extensive and systematic than real ethnography, gave him a push in that direction. Even in American society, the idea of doing the foreign and different as a means of describing, uncovering, or discovering reality is not uncommon. Investigative reporters go undercover to flesh out a religious cult or infiltrate the KKK. In law enforcement, undercover cops and narcs assume the identity of those they wish to apprehend, participating fully in their life, much as Al Pacino did in *Serpico*.

The news media now hire their own "experts," those who were or are actively engaged in a culture or position. These individuals use their familiarity and social intimacy to try to explain a newsworthy event, such as Desert Storm, political campaigns, even plane crashes. As I am writing these words, Alaska Air flight 261 has crashed into the Pacific a few miles from where I live. Major news stations, searching and grasping for an angle on the crash, interviewed current and former pilots to place us, the viewers—who have never been in or near a cockpit except to pass by it on our way to coach seating—in the cockpit for those last few moments before the plane plummeted into the Santa Barbara Channel. To the news stations, questions about responsibility, last-minute scenarios, and last-second dialogues were questions to which the viewing public anxiously awaited answers. Although none of these examples are ethnography—not even the undercover work—they reveal the fascination humans have with those who are not like us.

In the preceding chapter, Malinowski's fieldwork illustrated the unique and problematic nature of ethnography. In the following four chapters, I will briefly touch on those components, or features, of ethnography that Malinowski first encountered and that others have since experienced.

This chapter will introduce the nature of long-term fieldwork by describing

- participant observation,
- the relationship between fieldworker and cultural members,
- the social and physical parameters of where behavior is observed and participated in, or the "cultural scene,"
- the feelings of culture shock that all ethnographers experience, in some form or another,
- the necessity of building a mutually beneficial rapport with cultural members, and
- the amount of time invested in fieldwork.

These features are a recipe for orienting the fieldworker to the proper frame of mind. Understanding these foundational features will provide a good start to the ethnographic experience, an experience that will be professionally and personally satisfying and will challenge the ethnographer to examine his or her own cultural beliefs.

Participant Observation

The main fieldwork method in ethnography is participant observation. Ethnography is separated from other qualitative social science research methods by its emphasis on intensive, focused, and time-consuming participation and observation of the life of the people being studied. Ethnography is also, as anthropologist Alice Reich writes, an "oxymoron," a phrase that combines contradictory behaviors (Reich in Kutsche 1999, 6). Intent on becoming involved in the routine of life, Malinowski daily "wandered" through the predictable chores and subsistence activities of the islanders. His presence, after a while, became accepted. Malinowski was also around when unpredictable events occurred, allowing him a front-row seat to discover the eccentricities and happenings that make life interesting and real. While Malinowski participated, however, he made systematic observations of the events that swirled around him. Malinowski claimed that some events were so important that they defied recording through questioning or computing in documents. He felt that these events had to be observed in their occurrence and labeled them "the imponderabilia of actual life" (Malinowski 1984, 18). What Malinowski was after were the intangibles of human behavior, such as friendships, adherence to routine and schedule, the tone of conversations that were lost through questioning or interviews that lay outside the arena of inquiry and the daily life of the cultural members. Malinowski's participation was neatly wrapped up in the scope of his observation. Every ethnographer feels Reich's belief that participant observation mixes distinct and contradictory behaviors. After reading Malinowski's seminal work on the Trobriand Islanders, *Argonauts of the Western Pacific,* one cannot help but think that his method has been a successful venture. Only when perusing his diary do the difficulty and hardships encountered in participant observation become known.

Participation is an engrossing and daunting task that involves a time-consuming effort to establish rapport with a new "community" and learn how to act in that community so that the ethnographer is eventually accepted as part of the social landscape. While learning how to fit in, the ethnographer must also travel in the opposite direction, achieving a removal from the everyday existence that he tries so hard to assimilate and become immersed in. The ethnographer must develop a perspective that mediates his or her cultural background and that of the newfound cultural mates. The fieldworker notes the experiences on paper so that on return to the field notes in a year or so, back from the field and reading them in home or office, the ethnographer can produce an authentic and valid text.

Contemporary ethnography, especially that of interpretive or postmodern ethnography, is also concerned with the effect the ethnographer has on the culture being studied. Observation may only slightly affect cultural behavior and practices, but the participation of the fieldworker in the everyday life of the culture will definitely affect cultural behavior (see chapter 8). Narby (1998, 13) writes that since the 1960s, anthropologists "came to realize that their presence changed things." It is not too difficult to see that a foreign presence can at first affect a team or community, can disrupt the flow of normal social intercourse. But as Malinowski and every ethnographer since has discovered, the more time spent with the culture and the more participatory the fieldwork, the less intrusion is felt by the fieldworker and cultural members. For Malinowski, the adage of "seeing life through the eyes of the native," although questioned today by interpretive ethnographers for its veracity, speaks to the effort of the fieldworker to become culturally invisible by becoming culturally similar.

Entrance into the culture is always humbling. The process of gaining access into a culture foreign from the fieldworker demands that the fieldworker be immersed from the outset of the study. Losing the false confidence of presumed familiarity and adopting the humility of fieldwork means that nothing is known until learned from cultural members or experienced by the fieldworker. Experiencing this period of cultural education will ultimately provide a richer and more complete understanding in the completion of the ethnography. When the fieldworker is familiar with the culture and knowledge that defines culture members, a sense of comfort with the experiences lulls the fieldworker into a false sense of knowing. In many cases, entering with assumptions based on prior experience with that culture acts to blind the fieldworker to altered perspectives of those fundamental cultural truths that lay the foundation for behavior.

In work with recreational college-aged basketball players, my having played college basketball 10 years before the fieldwork colored and in a sense biased my perception of the initial cultural reality in a college recreational gym. I barged into the field site confident of my athletic and ethnographic ability. I felt that I was going to spend little time assessing the cultural ropes before getting to the heart of my fieldwork—observation, interviews, and life histories of my study mates. I quickly found that the type of basketball played and the cultural rules of performance and of accessing court time were far different from what I experienced growing up playing neighborhood games and organized basketball. I could have better used the time that I spent shaking these assumptions. At the heart of this entrance to a culture is the relationship of the fieldworker to the population at the beginning of fieldwork, *self* versus *other.*

Self Versus Other

The basic dichotomy of fieldwork is wrapped up in the Leví-Straussian binary opposition that seems to characterize cognitive comprehension of the universe that surrounds each of us. The world is both similar and different to us, and that extends to social interaction. We tend to interact most with those similar to us and far less frequently with those who, in some way or another, are different, either in physical appearances or in ethnic or cultural features. In many ways that is what defines and distinguishes culture from culture—shared perceptions of reality that spring from like-minded people.

At the birth of modern ethnography, Malinowski could easily discern himself from those he was studying. The Trobriand Islanders were physically different, lived in an environment dissimilar to Poland or London, and spoke a different language. Their actions and behaviors were predicated around livelihoods as fishermen and yam harvesters. Save for a few accounts of other white travelers, the islanders were largely unknown.

Malinowski's fieldwork, and the use of his diary, allowed him to participate in Trobriand culture yet still remain distant enough to maintain a comfortable illusion of social dichotomy of *self* versus *other.*

For the native is not the natural companion for a white man, and after you have been working with him for several hours, seeing how he does his gardens, or letting him tell you items of folklore, or discussing his customs, you will naturally hanker after the company of your own kind. (Malinowski 1984, 7)

Colonialism encouraged, even demanded, this perception of its administrators and those anthropologists doing fieldwork in cultures caught up in the web of colonialism. The colonial mind-set made it more difficult for anthropologists to cast off ethnocentrism. In a way, the participant-observation method of traditional ethnography was a contradiction in concepts: how much could self know other without losing self to other. In a nutshell, this has always been the curse of ethnography and cultural research in general—the tension created when describing what ethnographers do as a humanistic science. Narby calls participant observation "a dance on the edge of paradox" in which the anthropologist-ethnographer "plays the schizophrenic role of the player/commentator" (1998, 14). Here, the ethnographer is cursed with a dual purpose—to know the culture as a member while watching the culture as an observer, leading to the image of seeing yourself in a mirror, seeing yourself in a mirror, ad infinitum. Yet the concept of a schizophrenic as ethnographer is misleading; the ethnographer is not locked into this duality in the same way that a schizophrenic is joined to the whims of his or her disease. The ethnographer has more leeway in presenting experiences and observations of fieldwork, can step in and out of the roles of participant and observer, and can manage the flow of experience. Yet it is the relationship of self and other and how that relationship is managed through the period of fieldwork, and even beyond, that is crucial to successful ethnography.

In the last 40 years the world has shrunk to the size of the fiber-optic wires that transport images and text about any culture from innumerable Web pages to a computer screen. The differences encountered by Malinowski have been reduced by instantaneous access. The comfortable distance between self and other has become minimized. Those different live right at your back door in cyberspace. The ethnographer now commonly does fieldwork among those who are familiar. The assorted features of ethnicity and race, language, religion, origin, and so on fall prey to the 21st century boundaries of identity that revolve more around cultural roles, positions, vocation, class, gender, and alternate lifestyles. That is not to say that the more traditional features are not defining, but identity attribution has become far more complex.

In all of this change, the ethnographer has not gone without having methods questioned, even challenged (see chapters 6 and 9). But the traditional dichotomy has remained, in some ways, a constant. The role of the fieldworker, notwithstanding any other identity features brought to the study, will always, at least at first, separate the ethnographer from the other. For those already involved in sport studies, fieldwork will involve being *self* among *self*. In other words, participant observation may involve doing fieldwork with a group of athletes in a sport in which the ethnographer participated. Those interested in sport studies may already have an intimate knowledge of the sport and athletes through exposure in lived experience, if not from active sport participation.

The cyber revolution has hacked up distance between and brought information to our fingertips. Gaining knowledge is no longer the prime directive of ethnography as it was 100 years ago. The immediate goal of ethnography is understanding how this knowledge becomes an integral part of the identity of cultural members. In my work with sprinters, I discovered that identity of "sprinter" was encased within the domain of cultural knowledge that defined the culture of sprinters. Accessing this knowledge by sprinters or by a sprinting ethnographer lay in the interaction of cultural members. "Knowledge only becomes knowledge through the relations of cultural identities and this knowledge is made available through cognitive (mental) rules that are expressed in the order and arrangement of positions within an identity" (i.e., sprinter, football player, surfer, etc.) (Sands 1995, 20). In this look at ethnography, self becomes the tool for probing the knowledge of cultural identity, and other is the key to unlocking the cultural fountain of information.

In my studies of college recreational basketball players and college sprinters, *self* was opposed to *other* in stark, definitive ways. In both studies, the fact that I was white—in an otherwise black sport environment—proved to be a visible reminder of identity opposition. This was compounded by the fact that I was also a graduate student–graduate assistant and 10 to 15 years older than those I studied. Susan Brownell (1995), an elite heptathlete, spent a year competing for a Chinese university so that she could study gender order and the politics of the Chinese female body. She found a remarkably different reality for the Chinese female athletes than she was accustomed to in her experiences. Even though the sport was similar, the contrasting "universes" created a well-defined initial self-versus-other relationship. Journalist and anthropologist Mari Womack studied the Los Angeles Dodgers from the dugout, spending time during and after games. She experienced the workout, practices, and down time in ways not available to others. Her role as a reporter, as a female, and as an anthropologist rigidly defined this self-versus-other dichotomy. Belinda Wheaton (1997), already a windsurfer, labeled her position as a "complete" participant in her covert study of the windsurfing culture (see chapter 6). But Wheaton encountered more than the initial dimension of otherness, respective to athlete-ethnographer, because her gender also produced a measure of otherness in a male-dominated sport. In many ways the label of experiential may include not only fieldwork situations encountered by different ethnographers where the roles of other and self are filled with different identities but also different perspectives on cultural reality and the use of data in analysis.

Alan Klein, in his work on baseball (1997), acknowledged his qualities not only as an ethnographer but also as an Anglo, which distinguished him from the community of the baseball team. This led him to question the accuracy of his representation of their reality (see chapter 6 for a discussion of representation in ethnography), but he strongly asserted that he could later use to advantage this initial limitation based on distinctness to create channels of information flow.

Although self does finally come close to being other in the most extreme case of ethnography, or participant observation, the merging of identities can never be complete. Reflexive methodology, which has become the tool of choice by contemporary postmodernists and by those of many other emerging fields of study—feminist studies, interpretive studies, cultural studies, and so on—places the ethnographer as central to the fieldwork process and integral to data acquisition. Even as the central focus is on the narrative of the fieldworker, the separation of ethnographer and cultural members is implicit and continually understood by the active description of the experiences of the fieldworker.

de Garis (1999) suggests that the relationship between self and other is a natural outcome of research and that it should not be erased. He contends that during his fieldwork with boxers, his education and position as fieldworker nullified his ability to become a complete participant. To de Garis, becoming a complete participant would have created an unnatural or artificial environment, and his interest lay outside the scope of simply duplicating the cultural reality of boxing. Ben Pink Dandelion (1997) recounted his experience as an insider doing research on Quakers and balanced out the immediacy and familiarity of the field situation with the uncomfortable feelings of guilt about preying on friendships and a research protocol that snipped and tore at the fabric of his relationships with the Quakers (see chapter 6).

The acknowledgement that there exists a self and other may seem obvious, yet to fieldwork in contemporary society—both within and across cultures—this dichotomy can become blurred, even dissolved. The famous ethnographic film, *Trobriand Cricket: A Case Study in Culture Change,* presented an image of Trobriand cricket that was radically different from English cricket. The first part of the film was a history of how cricket arrived in the islands. The second part traced the evolution of the game from English cricket to the wild and woolly island form today, with many insights from island players and village elders who remembered the beginning of the Trobriand style. It was clear, even in this medium, that self was categorizing other and offering explanation. The last third was a view of a cricket game from how an American person would see the context, complete with music and a play-by-play announcer. This third segment was a clear example of self distinct from other, yet because of brevity and further concerns, the film stopped short of self distinct from other, yet knowing other. These different perspectives gave the viewer alternate looks at the phenomenon of Trobriand cricket. Like any ethnography, the ethnographic film has shortcomings—it offers a condensed view and is forced to select certain images as a perspective. A film accompanied by supplemental information could fill in the gaps and present a more complete picture.

The most inclusive perspective (derived from reflexion) is the ethnographer transformed into the cultural member, in this case athlete. This method is slightly different from Wheaton's approach, as she was a windsurfer before initiating her fieldwork. In this respect, self becomes other. Caught between the traditional goal of objectivity in classic ethnography and the need to distinguish self from other to delineate interpretation, the role of ethnographer as athlete attempts to produce intimate yet stark representations of cultural reality. Not without methodological pitfalls, this experiential ethnography opens up avenues of accessing cultural information not open to the observer and sheds new light on information accessed in the more traditional ways. Work by Brownell, Bolin, Granskog, Wheaton, Giulianotti, Armstrong, me, and a host of others offers exciting glimpses, and in many cases detailed looks, at cultural reality heretofore left to representations from interviews and observation (see chapter 9 for an in-depth look at this type of ethnography).

The nature of fieldwork is that subjects are not vials, atoms, or chemical compounds. They, along with the researcher, are humans. Although this makes fieldwork a complex process, it also makes for an exciting and rewarding experience. As in wintertime Chicago, the road to success in ethnography is often paved with the bumps and chuckholes of experience.

Cultural Scenes

Once settled in the field, the ethnographer begins to experience the first chaos of social interaction, actors flying through daily routines and special performances, all the while entrained in a system of ritual. If already famil- iar with the culture, as either an observer or a participant, the chaos will be more understandable to the ethnographer. Work of cognitive anthropolo- gists Frake, Goodenough, Spradley, McCurdy, and Keesing in the late 1970s and early 1980s generated the concept of "cultural scenes"[1] in ethnographic research. Analogized in some respect to the stage and acting, scenes are often repetitive, bounded, or discrete units of social interaction in which information is shared between participants. More than a location or even modes of information exchange between cultural members, a cultural scene is ultimately the specific knowledge used in cultural situations. To take this notion further, cognitive maps within a culture or individual chart out the operating rules of how members or identities should act. The map is also a key to how and where cultural knowledge is generated.

A large part of the early work of ethnography is the necessary legwork to uncover or discover these cultural scenes. This is not as time consuming or literal as it seems. All humans, ethnographers too, naturally exist in a fluid social environment where cultures at times intersect and interact. Humans also live primarily in one culture in which these cultural scenes play out repeatedly. At the extreme, I posit, along with others such as Frake, Keesing, and Spradley, that a cultural grammar exists in our minds to help us sort out these cultural scenes. Culture is composed of these often bounded units of social interaction.

The human behavior of sport plays nicely into this concept of cultural scenes. In my research, cultural scenes were cast as a gym, a track, a foot- ball field, and now a wave. To Belinda Wheaton, a cultural scene was com- posed of several windsurfing beaches along the Atlantic Ocean of the United Kingdom (1997). Alan Klein's (1988) and Anne Bolin's (1997) cultural scenes were weight gyms for their respective work on bodybuilders and bodybuilding competitions. In Klein's look at baseball in the Dominican Republic (1991), part of the fieldwork took place at Campos Las Palmas baseball academy and presented him with a bounded, closed cultural scene. Observation also occurred at the professional stadium, again representing a repetitive, bounded space. Dan Hilliard's and Jane Granskog's respective

A cultural scene of a windsurfing beach in the United Kingdom.

individual work on triathloning featured a moving cultural scene, tied not to a place but to a scene generated by social interaction of the runners. Because long-distance running requires individual training, it can be said that a cultural scene may have just one participant. David Howe's (1999) study on English football, derived from his position as trainer, produced scenes on the pitch and in the training rooms. Michael Silk's (1999) field-work on New Zealand's media coverage of the Commonwealth Games produced a cultural scene inside a television truck outside the athletic venues.

Primary scenes, perhaps a track or gym, can easily be determined, but secondary scenes—where smaller numbers of members participate—can be just as revealing and informative. Sport, like the subjects of most con-temporary ethnography, is a spot-specific behavior. Not isolated on a tropi-cal island as the work of Malinowski was, cultural research is now played out in a shotgun approach—cultures are found in certain places and times (see chapter 4 on culture as the ethnographic unit of study). Doing research on football produced three to four hours a day in a variety of cultural scenes: locker room, stadium, training room, film room, weight room, and bus rides to away games. As with Klein's work on baseball, in which research en-tailed a similar kaleidoscope of scenes, each scene had specific behavior

Santa Barbara City College Football Stadium, a football field's length away from the beach and surf. My home for two years.

A wave from Scorpion's Bay, Baja, California, is also a cultural scene.

Even the familiar—a playground in rural Iowa—can be a cultural scene.

and identity interaction, different coaches, a trainer, and a different group of players. Only rarely did a scene include all the players (or cultures). Other scenes were nights out barhopping with players or *Monday Night Football* at players' apartments. Each scene produced cultural knowledge that was invaluable in piecing together a culturally valid reality. In a more performance-based participant observation, in which the ethnographer becomes a participating cultural member, competency is not only knowing the rules that guide interaction in the scene but also being able to take part in the interaction in the culturally prescribed manner. In the case of sport, knowing the rules of the sport is only part of the equation. Being accepted as a participating member of that athletic culture by those already in the culture is another, more important element. Even in an observational role, in which the performance of the ethnographer is not tied to the field or track or gym, discerning scenes and understanding the interactional dynamics and rules that determine the nature of these dynamics is crucial to the construction of cultural reality. Despite the appearance of being anchored to a location or a piece of land, scenes can also be formulated to transcend time or place and can exist within a cognitive matrix of past interactions found in oral or life histories (see chapter 5 for a more thorough discussion of life history). Recounting the lifetime of an informant produces a cultural scene that exists only in the retelling of that lifetime. A life history produces cultural knowledge that is not tied to the present but breathes in its constancy over time and its manifestation in cultural scenes.

Cultural scenes are not necessarily confined to spatial locations or physically bounded areas. When dealing with the self-reflexivity or the narrative of the ethnographer (see chapters 6 and 9), cultural scenes can also be "locations" within the mental "spaces" of interactions and social relationships. This notion resonates with Bourdieu's idea of "ethnography working in fields which are constructed objects" (H. Barnard in Hughson 1998, 48).

Culture Shock

I remember vividly the first time a football coach called me a "pussy" for missing a block. I was just into my fieldwork on college football. As a 37-year-old college professor I had little contact with people in positions of authority in an environment that demanded physicality. It was not that I had never heard that word or a similar one in sport venues I participated in, but this was the first time I was so labeled in a formal, structured setting. "Sands, you pussy, quit blocking like a fag and hit him harder," was what the coach yelled. My teammates all started shouting at me to do the same. I became enraged at the situation and attempted to throw the most vicious block I could on my partner in the drill. All I could see was red, and I became somebody else for that moment. Of course, I threw a poorly executed block but managed to knock my partner off his feet. Just five minutes later, I wondered what had happened to change me into an alien, separated from my world of academics and classroom interaction. Later that night as I wrote my field notes on the experience of the day, I rationally concluded that I had experienced culture shock.

My lifelong participation in athletics had ill-prepared me for the violence and savagery of football and the language of such violence. No matter how much I prepared myself for an alternate cultural reality, it came not in an "ah ha" moment but repeatedly in a flood of senses, dissipating my cultural values of gender equality and antihomophobia. Bohannan and van der Elst (1999, 52) observe that "when an alien logic penetrates, when your habituated convictions and values are knocked into a cocked hat, the agitation you feel is called culture shock."

In almost every fieldwork situation, the ethnographer at one time or another comes face to face with behavior or sets of values and norms that threaten the sanctity of his or her cultural premises. In addition, shock takes on the added feeling of separation from those familiar and close to the fieldworker. Culture shock may be expressed in different ways for different people. For me in the football example, it was something visceral, an assault on the premises I had learned in graduate school and earlier in my family. It was the opposite of what I had experienced, violent and embracing the sense that might is right. For those involved in fieldwork in a foreign country and culture, shock may take the form of how others are treated, or their diet or religious beliefs. In the traditional ethnography, culture shock was to be experienced but minimized or even avoided. Some of the earlier ethnographers did not have teachers and mentors who had been fieldworkers, anthropology was still in its infancy, and culture shock was yet to be recognized for what it was. Malinowski's diary was his answer to handling the culture shock of living among the Trobriand Islanders.

In much of contemporary ethnography, fieldwork is done among those in the same culture, if not cultural group, as the ethnographer. Feelings of loneliness or separation from cultural kin may not take on the type of feelings experienced by those working thousands of miles from home. No matter the distance, being cast initially as *other* in the face of *us* creates feelings of distance, especially if participation is complete. Contemporary ethnography, while not encouraging or demanding the fieldworker to experience shock, expects the experience in a foreign culture to be a vital part of experiencing cultural reality. Successful ethnography seldom allows the fieldworker to skate through the experience without questioning and exploring the effect of participant observation on the fieldworker.

In my experience with the theoretical side of ethnography (Sands 1991, 1995, 1999b, 1999c, and n.d.), I have suggested that fieldwork is navigating through a series of doors or stages, each door offering greater insight into understanding cultural reality. Culture shock can take on the property of one of those doors. Faced with outrageous or cognitively challenging behavior, the fieldworker can decide that the dissonance is too debilitating and leave the field or accept the behavior and continue fieldwork. Through a period of painful introspection, fieldworkers may realize that their own values may offer the same sort of challenge to the "natives." In any case, if fieldwork is to continue, the fieldworker must reach a new sense of balance that leads to the realization, irrational or not, that the behaviors are consistent with the cultural values of those studied.

Traditional ethnography buried culture shock in the numerous pages of description and analysis. Fieldworkers used methodology, actual data gathering, to deflect, or even construct a barrier against, the anxieties and moral outrage experienced during fieldwork. Today, good ethnography includes the experience of culture shock and the effect it has on the fieldworker. This admission of shock and the description of the interaction between fieldworker and behavior becomes an integral part of retelling the "story" of ethnography. During my two seasons of football fieldwork, this sense of shock over graphic imagery of gender desensitivity and homophobia continually haunted me. For some, culture shock is an initial period of disorientation or short-term depression that somehow subsides as the fieldwork progresses. "I had periods of despondency, when I buried myself in the readings of novels, as a man might take to drink in a fit of tropical depression and boredom." (Malinowski 1984, 4) For others, however, shock is more long term. Instead of coming to terms with these periods, some fieldworkers submerge shock and even become numbed by the daily regimentation of experiencing life and observing it at the same time. But culture shock occasionally resurfaces. When that occurred in my football experience, I felt torn by the culture of football and what it at times represented. How as an anthropologist could I participate in a culture where these values propagate? After a while, I discovered that other players experienced the same disorientation off the field, but the immediacy and physicality of the football experience relied on such "values" to enforce perceptions of good and bad players.

Football was a goddamn violent game. To make the breakdown and buildup game work, primal feelings were appealed to by using graphic images of manhood. And this was accomplished by using stark, polarized dichotomies. Football was we versus them, we either win or lose, we played well or we sucked, we beat the guys or we got beaten. Football was a game played by men, for men. Either you were a man or not a man, or if you weren't a man, then you were a "pussy." (Sands 1999e, 93)

I had uncovered a cultural truth of football. Seeing how these values were integrated into cultural behavior and how they served the successful functioning of a football team helped with the dissonance I felt.

In another data entry, I wrote about undergoing this culture shock:

I can't remember how many times I was called a pussy for missing a block or dropping a ball after a hit. Suffice to say it was many. Not so much from the coaches, but from the players. When it came, it was meant. In the moment of execution, I was stripped of my person and identity and all that mattered was my ability. Did I block, did I catch. A man did, a pussy didn't. I remember times when, under my breath or out loud, I chastised a teammate for being nonchalant or not going all out and called him a fucking pussy or worse. In the heat of the moment, I bent under the weight of the culture. In the heat of the moment, screaming "pussy" at a player never felt more right. (Sands 1999c, 100)

Culture shock also affects the reader, although readers are less vulnerable to it. The reader has available a built-in defense or avoidance mechanism and can choose to skip a disturbing section, skim through it, or toss the book aside. Still, the reader faces the same disorientation and must grapple with the painful yet exhilarating feeling of expanding one's cultural horizons. Reading passages about men calling other men "pussies" or digesting text concerned with female circumcision in the Sudan may not carry the powerful imagery of experiencing it, but a sense of shock still occurs.

Because the social landscape has changed dramatically since the era of traditional ethnography and the Internet age has opened up otherwise alien cultures to both anthropologists and the public, culture shock is no longer as immediate and disorientating. Ethnography of sport is a relatively recent phenomenon, however, and fieldwork done in cultural situations such as the football field, Latin baseball leagues, a workout gym, a bodybuilding contest, or on the 8,000-foot-high running trails of Kenya represent novel situations. The degree of the fieldworker's involvement through participant observation will without a doubt produce periods of culture shock. Doing successful ethnography in any environment requires a successful negotiation through these cultural land mines. They may explode—no, they will explode—on the ethnographer, but learning will inevitably follow. Not attempting this navigation will surely deny learning and closet the ethnographer in the dark.

In summary, culture shock can be likened to growing through the teenaged years. As 13-year-olds, we all felt awkward, were self-conscious of our position in the scheme of things, and blushed a lot. To many, it seemed as if those feelings would never leave. Eventually, though never quickly enough, those feelings were replaced by a sense of competence, if not a feeling of belonging. As ethnographers, we enter the field coming from a culture where we are proficient cultural actors. Thrust into a situation where we are novices, we have to learn a new cultural code, or grammar. We can think back to the years when our bodies and hormones had no regard for our social and cultural comfort. Culture shock, like the teen years, eventually passes.

Rapport and Collaboration

Ethnography cannot be a successful research method unless the fieldworker develops rapport and friendship with the cultural members being studied. In his seminal work on interpretation in anthropology, "Deep Play: Notes on the Balinese Cockfight," Clifford Geertz (1973) describes an event that occurred early in his fieldwork in Bali that led to an establishment of rapport with the local villagers where Geertz and his wife were living. When they first arrived, the villagers treated the Geertzes with marked indifference. Several days later, the local police raided a cockfight where the Geertzes were present. Geertz and his wife fled the scene, along with the rest of the village, and were eventually detained by the police and asked about their presence at the cockfight. The village chief went to great lengths to defend the American couple, even going as far to say that they lived in the village and were unaware of the cockfight. Starting the next morning, Geertz found the invisibility and indifference replaced by acceptance and familiarity. "Getting caught, or almost caught in a vice raid is perhaps not a very good generalizable recipe for achieving the mysterious necessity of anthropological fieldwork, rapport, but for me it worked very well" (1973, 416).

In its simplicity, flushed from the theoretical and ethical implications of hegemony and colonialism, establishing rapport is something that all of us have been a part of on one side or the other of the process.

> quite naturally seek out the natives' society. . . . And by means of this natural intercourse, you learn to know him, and you become familiar with his customs and beliefs far better than when he is a paid, and often bored, informant. (Malinowski 1984, 7)

When I was young, I remember moving into a neighborhood in the Midwest. For a while, even in the neighborly, friendly Midwest, our family was considered outside the already established dynamics of interaction between the neighbors. It was only after time and effort on our part to ingratiate ourselves to them that we were accepted as one of the neighborhood. Acceptance followed after we loaned lawn and garden equipment, collected newspapers and mail while neighbors went on vacation, and went out of our way to be friendly. Having to overcome cultural barriers occurs all the time in social interaction. The ethnographer faces these same kinds of barriers when establishing an identity within the culture. As the ethnographer initiates this process, he and the cultural members know that the fieldworker will never truly become a part of the culture.

The fieldworker seeks knowledge that she will use to pursue science or provide a description for consumption by outsiders for benefit to the fieldworker. This multilayered relationship is fraught with difficulty, anxiety, self-doubt, and to George Marcus, *ethical ambiguity*. However the ethnographer faces problems that arise during the course of fieldwork, gaining and maintaining trust and friendly relations with the cultural members is a necessity. This task involves cultivating relations with prominent cultural members and then allowing their approval to seep down through the culture. Another important step is showing respect to cultural members and accepting the lifeways of the culture.

Establishing rapport is without doubt the most humbling experience undertaken by an ethnographer. In the beginning stages of research, the primary goal is to establish a relationship with the leading persons of that culture, those who Miller (1999) labels "gatekeepers—people who formally or informally control access to human or material resources to the group or

One of my best gatekeepers during football fieldwork, equipment manager Pat Aguilera.

University of Illinois sprint coach Willie Williams, first a gatekeeper, then a valued informant.

community." After establishing rapport with the gatekeepers, the ethnographer is then able to establish relationships with a range of subjects from across the social spectrum. In the past, these secondary and more long-lasting relationships centered on individuals who ethnographers have referred to as "informant."

American culture has attached a pejorative meaning to the label *informant*—narc, snitch, stooley, and so forth. In ethnography an informant is simply one who is in a good position to inform the ethnographer on a variety of features of that particular culture. Many ethnographers now are trying to get away from the term *informant*. Some use *teacher* in its place. Initially, the role of informant is predicated on a recognized leadership role in the culture, but as time passes, others may become important in addressing specific cultural features or less recognized views. In his research on football hooliganism, Giulianotti labeled the method of gaining access to informants as *snowballing,* seeking introductions to cultural members, who in turn introduce the ethnographer to others, who in turn introduce others. Over time, and with luck, access to cultural members capable of producing pertinent information increases. "Snowballing may take years when starting with someone on the indices of the research group and wider society, or at the metaphorical base of the subculture's pyramid of status" (Giulianotti 1995, 7). During my sprinting research, I counted each of the small population as an informant, but after a year, I ended up being roommates with two of the sprinters, and they become an important channel and source of cultural information.

Ethnographers historically have helped ease the process of mining for cultural information by offering gifts and beneficial exchanges to the cultural members. Malinowski provided tobacco, a valuable and scarce resource to Trobriand Islanders, for information and interviews. Often unstated but left to the ethnographer to discover are the expectations of the cultural members for contributing their knowledge to the ethnographer. In my work on basketball players and college football players, the gift of beer—culturally relevant and appropriate to the demographics of the population—was given in exchange for interviews. Perhaps more binding than the gift of beer was my complete participation as one of the group of athletes. In a sense, this legitimized their perceptions of the importance of the behavior they spend countless hours practicing.

In my work with college sprinters, I quickly found that a large part of the complex association that developed between the sprinters and me was predicated on a teacher-student relationship, me filling the role of the student. Knowledge was disseminated in a variety of contexts. At first, the most prominent method featured the sprinters lecturing me on the finer points of competition and training. I felt as if I were back in college, the lecture hall replaced by a track. Although the sprinting team was small—only 12 members per year with little change over the three years of my fieldwork—I was fortunate enough to include all the team as informants. My football research was constructed around a population that exceeded 100 players and coaches. In this case, informants were few, and I established rapport with those willing to play that role. At first, those I sought for information were players of ability or leaders. Over time, a few of them remained informants, but time allowed me to discover not only those who were the most knowledgeable but also those who represented different personalities. I thus had access to a broad spectrum of players and knowledge. Of course, I became close to some players during research, and they provided me with information.

Surf informants become surf friends at Hobson's Point.

In research that I labeled earlier as experiential ethnography, based on the intense participation of the ethnographer (see chapter 9 for a discussion of this method), rapport was also based on my being a competitor, filling the same role as the athletes did. This increased the familiarity between the athletes and me and eased my transition from outsider to insider. A certain amount of trust flowed from their realization that I was experiencing the same pain of training, anxiety of competition, and sacrifice of time and effort that they were. In a way, I was earning the right to access their knowledge and use it to further my fieldwork.

In his study of baseball in the border towns of Laredo, Alan Klein built rapport in a variety of ways, some based on features unique to him and others carved out of his fieldwork. In the Latin atmosphere of machismo, Klein's gender and his past background in baseball provided common concerns and appreciations. This, combined with his ability to match them in their conditioning program, produced a respect "along basic machismo-hypermasculine lines that I gladly, if politically incorrectly, took since it enabled a basis of sharing (male) culture" (Klein 1997, 265). In addition, sharing long bus rides and life on the road impressed the Tecos players and paved the way to a comfortableness expressed in joke telling at Klein's expense, which included him in the experience. Klein found humor to be a doorway to his success in fieldwork.

Collaboration

Recently, some ethnographers have replaced this notion of rapport with the idea of collaboration. In a sense, the ethnographer and informants join to forge a relationship in which information and knowledge is transferred. This idea involves bringing the informants into the process at varying levels of cooperation. As part of the process of accessing cultural reality in each of my four studies, I cognitively challenged my informants to describe and explain behavior necessary for functioning in that culture. In the end, the representation of cultural reality was produced by more than just my voice. In planned and impromptu meetings of "playing" minds, I would test my experiences by asking them questions designed to elicit information about whether they were undergoing similar experiences. These sessions often produced moments of realization about the meaning of experience, not only in me but also in others.

Collaboration does not always involve the establishment of an active social and physical interaction between ethnographer and cultural members. Mazer's work (in press) on professional wrestling involved her desire to be invisible to her informants, watching and note taking on the sidelines. In such a masculine sport, to Mazer, her gender and profession as scholar would be effectively minimized. In an interesting twist, one of her subject-informants, Larry de Garis (now a professor at Washington State University), argues that Mazer was never invisible and instead her experience was part of the lived experience of the wrestlers. In fact, her observation played into the necessary and crucial aspect of wrestling as a performative game: "Ironically, Mazer is a greater part of the game than she thinks, as a spectator . . ." (de Garis 1999, 69).

In the ethnography of performance (sport, theater, cinema) to de Garis, both the performers and observers share in creating texts (see chapter 6 on writing ethnography). Each party can tell the story through the text (de Garis 1999, 69). Does that mean, as collaboration might be understood, that the text created becomes a benefit to both ethnographer and cultural members? Today, with so much of cultural heritage and tradition becoming a limited and often protected resource, the ethnographer must not only enlist the aid of cultural members but also actively engage them in producing an accurate representation of cultural reality. Collaboration extends beyond the actual fieldwork. A few ethnographers have enlisted the aid of informants in writing the ethnography. In his ethnography of a gay Jewish temple, Shokeid (1997) encountered difficulty when an informant became a silent coauthor. Spirited debate occurred about the perception of Shokeid and his informant's reality of social relationships between temple members.

No matter the difficulty, the audience of ethnography is no longer strictly academic. The subjects of the ethnography increasingly demand that it also be addressed to them.

Time: The Great Equalizer

If there is one area in which ethnography resembles the empirically driven physical sciences or the more time-specific social sciences, it is the amount of time spent doing research. Years can be spent working in a lab or excavating a ruin or an early hominid site in Kenya. Many more years can be spent looking for that site or polishing the hypothesis that will lead to the discovery of DNA. The need for good old-fashioned fieldwork has not changed. Among traditional ethnographers, Malinowski spent the better part of three years in the Trobriand Islands, Franz Boas spent a greater part of two decades working with the Kwakutl on the northwest coast, and Ruth Benedict spent many seasons working with indigenous tribes in the Southwest.

Good sport ethnography demands the same expenditure of time. Whether it be participant fieldwork with a team or group of athletes, fieldwork involving observation of athletes on and off the field, or even a series of formal interviews, time spent involves months or years as well as consecutive hours of the day. For this type of qualitative research to work, a relationship of familiarity, trust, and comfortableness must be reached with the cultural members. This rapport does not occur overnight or after a one-hour interview. In my work on sprinting, I described time spent in the field as a way of "knowing" faces. "Faces would leave, but as the days raced into weeks and months and finally years, there would remain three distinct black faces, of which all the other faces would revolve around. A triangle would become a circle of speed" (Sands 1995, 2).

Examples of lengths of fieldwork highlight the extended duration of the ethnographer in the field. Annie Bolin spent five years of participant observation with competitive bodybuilders in two locales. Alan Klein's similar work on bodybuilders covered eight years and included field stints of from one month to one year in four locations. Belinda Wheaton spent two years of fieldwork with windsurfers. Klein's work on Laredo baseball covered four seasons south of the border during which he made seven trips, ranging from one week to five weeks, with five of those trips occurring in the 1993 and 1994 seasons. Archetti's (1997) work on Argentinian football covered over 10 years of observation and interviewing.

In my four studies, fieldwork included three years with sprinters, one year with rec basketball players, and two years with college football players. Currently, I am in the third year of work on surfers. In comparison with most ethnography dealing with sport, my fieldwork has been consecutive, with the majority of research occurring in one locale—a rec gym, a track, a football stadium, and now a surfbreak. I was (and am) part of daily interaction. In this way an unbroken continuity is established between ethnographer and cultural members.

Many times this type of immersion is not possible or feasible, and the ethnographer chooses to do periods of extended fieldwork. Klein makes the case that to his baseball subjects in Laredo he was—through his shorter and repeated trips to Laredo over a period of four years—perceived as "somehow more real, a person who will return continually" (1997, 260). With each returning visit, trust grows and information becomes more accessible. In this way, the ethnographer does not grow bothersome, and subjects anticipate his or her presence. Malinowski suggested taking vacations from fieldwork. Like Klein, he found that the benefits were realized not only by the cultural members (or "natives") but by the ethnographer as well. In a sense, repeated shorter fieldwork periods allow the ethnographer to recharge fieldwork batteries.

Educators often find it difficult to arrange for the time necessary to conduct extended fieldwork in areas other than where they work or teach. Klein's trips to Laredo and the Dominican Republic were an example of maximizing fieldwork on a budget of limited time. For research like Bolin's bodybuilding, Granskog's triathloning, or Wheaton's windsurfing, being able to conduct fieldwork in the area where professional and personal lives are rooted provides the opportunity for an unbroken period of fieldwork. For my work, my professional life and fieldwork were in the same location, allowing for one long, continuous period of fieldwork. Sprinting and football consist of various seasons—off-season, summer, and the competitive season—so fieldwork covered different types of training and cultural scenes. In addition, for each season, new faces augmented the returning faces to provide a fresh perspective on cultural makeup, a chance to reflect on microunits of cultural change, and a greater chance to observe different nuances of cultural behavior. Notwithstanding the obvious limitations of profession, travel, and time, doing good ethnography requires a commitment from the ethnographer to spend an extended period in the field.

Another type of ethnography is described by Alan Klein as "git it and go." This method, due to expediency and pressure to produce a product, uses a shotgun approach. Cultural research groups, government agencies, and educational organizations now use this research tool. The ethnographer quickly delves into the culture looking for a short list of features or behaviors, executes some participant observation, identifies informants, and conducts formal interviews with a list of arranged sets of questions. Results are written up in a timely fashion, usually in a period of days or a week or two, and then submitted to the requesting party. The brevity and single-minded focus reflect the urgency of those organizations, which require for their success production of a product in a short time. It is ironic that ethnography, which traditionally has required a commitment to years of time in the field, has captured the fancy of American business and government, organizations that work in units of days and weeks (chapter 10 explores the use of this type of ethnography in a sport-related field).

Concluding Remarks

This chapter has, I hope, laid the foundation for ethnography by providing brief explanations and examples of important features of participant observation, such as the breadth and scope of fieldwork, the effect of fieldwork on the ethnographer, cultural scenes or units of fieldwork, establishing beneficial and respectful relationships with cultural members, and the cost in time and effort of fieldwork to the ethnographer. If you take anything away from this preview of fieldwork, it should be that ethnography cannot be accomplished without a comprehensive investment on the part of both the ethnographer and those chosen to be studied. If anything, ethnography is a two-way street. The following chapter explores the concept of culture as it relates to defining the population under study. Traditional concepts of culture stressed the foreign and exotic; now the culture concept includes the pedestrian and familiar. Certain features that characterize human cultural groups are found in both a culture of athletes and a culture of Trobriand natives.

Endnotes

1. See Sands 1991 for a more thorough discussion of this concept and application to my research on track and field.

Chapter 4

Culture and Ethnography

Cultures can have no "natural" boundaries but only those that people (anthropologists as well as others) give them.

—Christopher Brumann, *Current Anthropology*

I mplicit in the notion of the outsider-insider or us-them dichotomy is the mental construction of behavioral boundaries that separate distinct groups or populations—the ethnographer's group and those being studied. For fieldwork, even if the ethnographer is a member of that group, the role that is being played out in relation to fieldwork creates separation, and the process of research slowly diffuses that boundary. But there is another way of looking at these distinct entities—as *cultures,* distinct and drawn together by common beliefs, behaviors, and traditions. The concept of culture, both as a panhuman phenomenon (humans have a capacity to learn new tricks) and as a homogeneous group of people, was essential to the growth and maturity of 20th century anthropology. The concept of culture also found its way into other social sciences over the last 50 years. Today, a concept that once was applied to describe a people is now used in ways unrelated to the holistic designation of unique traits, behaviors, language, and so forth. Culture is used to refer to larger segments (Western or African culture), buyers or age generations (Generation X or the boomers), alternate lifestyles (gay culture), sociological reference (a culture of violence or a culture of pain), a distinct attitude (pop culture), or, as used in this book, a culture of athletes or even sport. The use of this label or concept has flooded our thinking. In an ethnographic sense, however, contemporary usage has diluted the meaning of culture and posed difficulty in defining exactly who or what is being studied. In addition, certain features or traits can be attributed to a culture by the nature of its existence. This becomes important in fieldwork and understanding.

In this chapter, the concept of culture will be looked at as an important element in doing good sport ethnography. No one would question the need of the ethnographer to define a group of athletes, coaches, or parents as an entity, bounded by common behavior, common goals, and perhaps even common language. Gary Alan Fine wrote an ethnography of Little League baseball, *With the Boys,* and concentrated on one team of players. Coaches, umpires, and parents also populated the study. Fine dealt mostly with the players, and the reader could get a sense of these 12-year-old players forming a group of youthful athletes who acted alike. Yet Fine could have also made the distinction that the entire experience created a culture of Little League, which would also involve coaches, parents, and officials. In this chapter, the concept of culture will be seen as part of the human experience. Whether that culture is an island people or a team of pubescent baseball players, the ethnographer must define boundaries, describe collective behavior, and explain symbols and labels.

This chapter will present a brief history of the use of culture. Currently, much discussion is occurring about the traditional meaning of culture placed in a contemporary context. Many, such as the postmodernists, favor dropping the use of culture as a unit of meaning and study. They argue that culture is a mental construct of the ethnographer, not the people. To postmodernists, culture becomes a tool for a Western science, helping to maintain a hegemonic order in world relations (see chapter 6 for a discussion of postmodernism and positivism). Yet there is still a need—in and out of academia—to address the notion of distinct groups of people, complete with their own identities. Even in its perceived imperfectness, the notion of culture is pervasive.

What actually defines culture, however, is problematic and an active concern of cultural researchers. It is certainly an abstraction, recognized and applied in a mentalistic "formula," but that formula is calculated differently from group to group. In this context, the notion of idealism (heritage of ideas that transcend people, place, and time) versus realism (acquired habits, customs, and institutions) will be discussed. Another view centers on a cognitively based concept of culture. In a sense, cultural behavior can be thought of as public representations and symbols of what is in the head of cultural members. There exists a device in the mind that acquires cultural behavior. The output from this device (behavior) is supported by a knowledge domain of information and knowledge available to cultural members. Cultural behavior is then rule-governed and generated through a process in which others' behavior is inputted into the acquisition device and processed through the knowledge structure.

In the end, the notion of culture will be retained and applied to groupings of people that do not fit into the traditional one people, one culture mode. Specific to this notion, the ethnographer can elicit, distinct to a culture, a pervasive cultural reality, specific cultural knowledge, and shared cultural behavior. The ability to frame these features in a bounded entity or culture represents a pragmatic way of looking at a concept that has merit in today's changing world but has a difficult meaning to pin down. It is this view of culture that allows an ethnographer to make the statement that "sport reflects culture."

In brief, this chapter will include

- the traditional meaning of culture,
- the concept of culture today,
- realism versus idealism,
- rule-governed culture,
- the culture of athletes,
- cultural knowledge, and
- cultural reality.

Traditional Meaning of Culture

Culture as a concept has changed little over the last 125 years, when Edward Tylor first defined it in his 1871 landmark work, *Primitive Culture.* "[Culture is] that complex whole which includes knowledge, belief, art, morals, law, custom and any other capabilities and habits acquired by man as a member of society." (Tylor 1871, 1) How the concept has been applied, however, has gone through several changes.[1] From its origins amidst the inherent racism of 19th century biological determinism, culture came to counteract the use by physical anthropologists of biological races to index distinct human groupings. These early evolutionists, fueled by a social Darwinism and convinced of the superiority of the white Europeans and descendants, felt that by accurately identifying "races of man" they would also be able to link languages and customs to physical races. Tylor's definition flew in the face of determinism. At the turn of the century, under the tutelage of Franz Boas, anthropologists were spreading out over the world to collect evidence discounting determinism and instead highlighting the cause of differentiation between humans—in diverse beliefs and practices—as one of social learning, not biology. Bronislaw Malinowksi's belief that humanity shared the same kinds of cultural institutions (marriage, religion, economy, etc.), or universals, along with Boas's theory that all humans belonged to the same panhuman race, propelled ethnography—and its unique ability to document the diversity of human behavior—into the forefront as a tool of the science of culture.

Anthropologists following in Boas and Malinowski's footsteps, such as Margaret Mead and Ruth Benedict, produced volumes of ethnography that fed a growing knowledge of the orderly, predictable customs and practices of non-Western, or tribal, societies. After spending long periods with foreign peoples learning the language and customs, ethnographers developed a perspective that became known as *cultural relativism*. Not making quick judgments on the different behavior and customs observed, but considering the role and context of such behavior and customs, this relativism grew to be the cornerstone of 20th century ethnography.

This perspective was in direct contrast to the beliefs of missionaries and colonial administrators. To them, tribal societies were primitive, prisoner to customs and traditions that made up a cultural jail. Cultures were seen as holistic and sharply bounded entities. There was no hesitation in moving in and subverting long-standing tribal cultural practices and replacing them with those more to their liking. Yet, in some cases, cultural tradition did not die out but through a process of syncretism (changes and modification) became reflected through alternate channels. This was the case of Trobriand cricket.[2] Trobriand Islanders (who inhabited a group of islands in Melanesia) had their practice of warfare and raiding, along with the magic and traditions that were integral to that warfare, squelched by missionaries and later by colonial administrators. The islanders were introduced to games and sports, such as soccer and running, as a substitute for war, but it was British cricket that they embraced. It was not long before the sport had been transformed into something that hardly resembled cricket played in the mother country. Villages traveled during the yam-harvest season to play other villages, and the sport became part of the larger Trobriand system of competition, or *kayasa*. Not limited to a certain number, teams featured entire villages as players. The sport also became infused with the rituals and magic that were once an important part of warfare. In a way, the sport of cricket became more a public performance—complete with chants, dances, and a reservoir for tradition—than a competition that fit the Western notion. Although outstanding performances by players are rewarded with gifts of tobacco, the outcome of the match is always in favor of the home team.

With the demise of colonialism and a changing world order came disillusion with the theory that cultures were distinct and bounded groupings. Ethnographers were prone to produce research that reified the ideal of cultural conformity, reducing a group of people to a body that shared everything from beliefs, values, and practices to even a point of view. Could one village, one neighborhood, a church, or a team of roller-hockey players be synonymous with an entire culture? In the last 40 years, imperialism has been replaced by a world that no longer can be segmented into neat little packages of cultural identity. Homogeneity has been replaced by heterogeneity. Boundaries are less distinct. To ethnographers and the people being studied alike, questions of who will draw the boundaries and where they will be drawn are not easily answered.

Culture Concept Today

The culture concept has withstood many evaluations over the last century, and core features have survived this tumult. These core essentials include learned behavior acquired through being a part of a culture and expressed in customs, habits, and practices. Other features include ideas and traditions that supersede or are independent of cultural members over time or through space. Still, there are those who would also incorporate material items produced by cultural members to be a part of culture. Others find the label *culture* so loaded with the baggage of colonialism—and consider it a tool used by a capitalistic world to support a hegemonic class order—that the concept brings more harm than good.[3] The new millennium ushers in an ironic juxtaposition of traditional and postmodern views on the culture concept. Unwilling to drop a concept so important to ethnography and anthropology, many doing cultural research attempt to fit the notion of culture to contemporary reality.

Culture Lost, Culture Found

Anthropology no longer lays sole claim to the concept of culture—other disciplines have become conscious of the culture concept. The concept has also reached beyond the borders of academia.

Suddenly people seem to agree with us anthropologists; culture is everywhere. Immigrants have it, business corporations have it, young people have it, women have it, even ordinary middle-aged men have it, all in their own versions. . . . We see advertising where products are extolled for a "bed culture" and "ice cream culture," and something called "the cultural defense plea" is under debate in jurisprudence. (Hannerz 1996, 30, in Brumann 1999, 9)

The irony is that as cultural researchers question the veracity and validity of the culture concept, some even suggest discarding the notion altogether (Brumann 1999). Both postindustrial society and the societies once dismantled by colonialism are embracing the notion of belonging to a culture. This move is fueled by the desire of many to see themselves as different in a world that encourages being different. Indigenous peoples like the Australian Aborigine, the Maori, and the Native American find it valuable, in both spirit and economy, to proclaim themselves a culture.

This development was never more apparent than during the 2000 Sydney Summer Olympics, which featured the exploits of 400-meter champion Cathy Freeman. In winning, she became the symbol of the Aborigine, long suppressed and discriminated against by the Australian government and Australian society. Her exploits were encased in the overall drama—or perhaps it was the drama of their history being encased in the Games—that was living testimony to both Australia and the world of what is was like to be Aboriginal.

Nations may attempt to create a culture that coincides with political boundaries, as South Africa did with apartheid and the assignment of indigenous peoples to "homelands." In extreme cases, nations denied the existence of differentiated and overlapping cultures and manufactured a culture to rationalize to outsiders mistreatment of traditional groups. What used to be an identity has become a tool for situating an identity in today's political and economic nexus. In the Olympics, Cathy Freeman, in a twist of irony, was claimed by Australia as symbol of cultural and national celebration.

It may be easier to define what a culture is *not* instead of what it is. A culture is *not* a big thing that can do things; it is an abstraction of both ethnographer and members. A culture cannot be driven like a car, seen like a forest, or scored as a goal or touchdown is. But a culture can be visualized as patterns of behavior that are recognized and claimed by a certain group of people. It could be construed as being made up of traits that are part of a cultural tool kit that can do things. In effect, a culture exists in the minds of those who belong. Thus one can speak of the Japanese culture in the same breath that one describes a culture of athletes—each owns a distinct mental picture of their culture, which is translated into a way of doing things. A culture does not own these patterns; members learn them through cultural interaction and behavior. The image of a culture often exists when members are faced with those not included in that culture. A culture can still be thought of as holistic, as in the case of Japanese culture, but culture is often transitory and reoccurring, apparent and acknowledged in contexts that appear and reappear on the radarscope of social interaction.

Idealism Versus Realism

A major philosophical concern of cultural researchers today is the notion of idealist and realist views of culture. Traditionally, cultures have been infused with a transcendent quality that harbors a reality that can exist independent of cultural members. This reality is a function of shared knowledge that living cultural members can access and that is reborn in generations after people pass on. In essence, cultures have a personality that can be thought of as being shaped to a sum of ideas and beliefs, translated into mental representations, and then transcribed into cultural or behavioral representations such as ritual, cultural practices, and public opinion. This sum is shared across the culture. In other words, consensus of members defines a culture.

Realists have a different concept of culture. Culture is learned or acquired behaviors, habits, customs, and beliefs. It is not so much those beliefs and customs that interest realists; it is the process of learning that designates culture. Realists "track the lived histories" (Aunger 1999, 100) of the cultural representations (derived from the mental representations) as they evolve from one form to another. In this process of tracking representations, ethnographers attempt to learn why this process of evolution or cultural selection—of picking or choosing a belief over competing beliefs—takes place and then uncover the forces that invite or limit social access to representations.

In the end, both views of culture operate with common understandings, such as what makes up cultural knowledge, how that knowledge is passed on, and how the representations that exist in the minds of cultural members can be delineated from the cultural behavior and material manifestations observed by the ethnographer.

Culture in the Head

At the heart of the current definition of culture is the view that its genesis is in the human mind. How we as culture-bearing humans access our surroundings and turn that information into representations plays a large role in guiding ethnography. Proponents of a cognitive-based view of culture claim that what we define as culture "exists in the head" (D'Andrade 1995) and the only way to get at this mental image is through the representations, or symbols, that are expressed in cultural interaction and behavior. The goal of ethnography is to comprehend what is in the head by observing and experiencing the symbolic, behavioral, and material representations.

Underlying this model of a mental culture is the existence of holding tanks of cultural knowledge—everything one needs to know to be a member of that culture. The meaning of these representations and symbols are based on these tanks of knowledge, which are available to and accessed by cultural members. Acceptable and unacceptable cultural behavior is then generated from the interaction between cultural knowledge and cultural members (see the later sections "Culture of Athletes" and "Cultural Identity" for an example of this orientation). What finally come out of this swirl of mentalistic imagery and observable behaviors are symbols and public representations—things people say, make, or otherwise make publicly available, more or less. Ethnography is concerned with the visible and expressed. But the ultimate goal, not often fully realized, is to get at the conception of those representations. Public symbols and representations are not at all the same as what people believe, know, understand, or otherwise have in mind. We commonly utter cliches and platitudes that we know are only rough approximations of our actual ideas about whatever the subject may be. Much of ethnography is trying to get at the representations of what cultural members have in their heads through the things people say and do. So, of course, we put that in the ethnography. Of course, different cultural members say different things. To find out what people have in their heads, however, is more difficult because what someone says is not the same as what he or she tries to say, or what he or she knows, believes, and understands. In essence, what we say and do is a result partly of what we experience and partly of what we know.

For example, if I asked a sprinter how he felt about running a 400 as compared with running a 100-meter race right after he ran a 400, the reply might fall along the lines of how the 400 is painful and a "bitch" to run. If I probed further, at a time off the track or removed from the experience (if not the memory) of the race, the sprinter might respond differently, couching his answer in terms of the feeling of triumph on winning or the high that comes from a successful race. Both answers, at the time, reflect the sprinter's perceptions and feelings, yet relying only on what is said at the time does not accurately reflect what is, or will be, in the sprinter's head at some point in the future.

In a way, the observations and experiences of the ethnographer, like those of the cultural members, can be thought of as mental orderings. Unique behavior, ritual, and public opinions are representations of these orderings and can be thought of as part of culture. Material items such as dress, tools, modes of transportation, Nike basketball shoes, or Yater surfboards are material representations of culture as well. How all these representations are sifted through cultural interaction, shaped and formed by cultural members, and then passed back and forth is also a part of culture. What is in the head of cultural members is sometimes difficult for the ethnographer to decode at first, but it becomes easier as the ethnographer becomes familiar with the representations, symbols, and behavior of the culture. In many circumstances, decoding the response or behavior of cultural members will produce only partial meaning and understanding, but that is the nature of prediction when dealing with humans rather than atoms.[4]

A Culture by Any Other Name Is a Culture

The culture concept was fundamental to the birth of anthropology. Despite dramatically changing world orders, it remains today the fundamental rallying concept. In its stability it has become an attractive concept to others wishing to study the diversity that makes up human populations. The icebergs that were cultures once isolated and defined by ethnographers are now melting into an ocean driven by currents unknown 100 or even 50 years ago. The early researchers saw cultures of the world as floating islands that occasionally went bump in the night. Researchers today see cultures driven by these newer currents, pared down to just parts of islands as changing world conditions have dashed cultures into each other. The pace of life has accelerated for all human populations, and the prophecy that no man is an island has never been more true than it is today. Cultures can now be found within cultures. They are no longer tied to a geographical location but exist in a variety of locations bound together by common behavior and beliefs.

The traditional cultural holism once anchored to ethnic or racial groups has recently been discarded by a number of cultural researchers (see chapter 6 on postmodern thought in ethnography). In today's Internet society, individuals can produce a designer culture that is a collection of traditions with the available global buffet thrown in. Ironically, even as many cultural boundaries dissolve or are redrawn, the global inundation of diversity threatens to swallow up the ethnic solidarity that many contemporary activists defend from outside forces.

As Brumann suggests, discarding a concept that has such a profound effect on both academic and lay people is nearly impossible and even counterproductive. It is possible to retain the features once applied to distant foreign and exotic peoples and apply them to the world today. In the end, defining culture is problematic; understanding what makes up a culture is not. A sprint team of 12, a football team of 65, a West Coast surfing population of hundreds of thousands—all three, I will suggest in the next section, can be thought of as cultures.

Culture of Athletes

At least in anthropology, the impetus for wrestling with the meaning of culture and what exactly a culture is stems from the traditional usage of holistic application to groups of people that have different languages, dress, customs, and environments. Though postmodernists and others argue that holism does not adequately reflect reality, it is hard to argue that an anthropologist or a traveler to Japan does not experience a Japanese culture. Despite the influence of television and a global economy, powerful traits and patterns of behavior still distinguish groups of people. The problem is coming up with an agreement between the ethnographer and the cultural member about what is included in the culture and where to draw the elusive boundaries to form the culture.

As cultural research follows the change in social and ethnic relations around the world, overemphasizing the ethnic cultures and underemphasizing the emergence of late 20th century cultures such as "gender, age, regional, professional and class cultures" (Brumann 1999, 12) will only serve to create greater diversity and meaning for the concept. To say that a Native American culture and a culture of sprinters are the same is unrealistic. Even without a background in cultural research, one can at least intuitively know the difference, if still unable to explain it. Identification of a culture of sprinters, however, is certainly valid. The features that pertain to common behavior, traditions, and knowledge are found in sprinters. Several important elements seem to be at work in defining sprinters, or any other population of athletes, as a culture.

There is a culture of football players, and here we are sharing the experience.

Common Behavior

First, after doing any amount of fieldwork, one can identify social behaviors that are common to sprinters and less common or nonexistent in other groups of athletes and nonathletes. Out of these behaviors come rituals and practices that are repeated constantly, reinforcing the notion of shared behaviors. In other words, to be a sprinter, one has to act like a sprinter. Sprinters everywhere intimately know many of these sprinting behaviors, no matter what affiliation or level, from high school to Olympic hopefuls. Warm-up drills, workout schedules, mental preparation, diet, and so forth can be thought of as a selection of these common behaviors. Some behaviors exhibited by the University of Illinois sprint team, however, were unique to them.

An example of an "Illinois" behavior was based on a fall preseason workout that took place at a clearing of parklike land adjacent to the university president's home. The area included a rather steep hill and a 400-meter loop that circled the rise of land (the highest point of natural elevation in the flat sea of corn that made up the experimental ag fields to the south of the campus). We dubbed the monster the "Hill," and after a brisk two-mile run to the park, drills, and 10 hill climbs up the front of the incline, we sprinted two loops, each separated by five minutes of rest. In the heat of Indian summer, weary, rubbery legs gave way to heaving stomachs. After the second loop, it seemed like hours before we could stagger the two miles back to the locker room. We did this workout no more than eight times each fall, but it spawned collective feelings of dread that intensified as the workout drew closer, elation when a workout was completed, mythlike stories of performances, and a bond that drew us together as a team. For some of the sprinters, the freshmen and transfer students, being a part of the Illinois sprint squad was a new and at times scary proposition. This type of fall workout is not just an Illinois workout, but the Hill and all it stood for was a symbol that was distinct to Illinois sprinters.

My research focused mainly on this group of sprinters, but it has application to the culture of sprinters at large. The idea of a strict homogeneity of behavior defining a culture is not applicable in today's world—intracultural variation can be great and still not affect general behavioral patterns of that culture.

I had a chance to spend three months training with and helping to coach the Saudi Arabian Olympic sprinters in the summer of 1988 before they went to Seoul, South Korea. Intercultural variation was never so evident in behavior off the track. But the Saudi on-track and training behaviors were similar to those I had observed and experienced with the Illinois sprinters. I had little difficulty expressing how both groups of sprinters fell neatly into a bounded entity of the culture of sprinters.

Shared Boundaries

Even as cultural boundaries weaken or are redrawn, the notion of boundaries is still translated into mechanisms that include cultural members and exclude those who are not members. In an elite sport culture, this membership is based on several features: skill, ability to withstand pain, a proficient work ethic, and so on (Sands 1991, 1995). Even in recreation-based cultures, such as running clubs, bowling leagues, windsurfers, and the like, certain features or elements act to define who is and who is not a member. Subtle and not-so-subtle tests become means by which membership is validated. During my sprint research, several people at different times joined the team in hopes of competing. Because the coach did not cut sprinters—he was fond of saying that it was better for those who could not compete at this level to realize it themselves—the marginal sprinters were never really considered part of the team. Eventually, their performance and behavior did not align with those expected of the sprinters, and they stopped coming to practice. How those who were part of the team interacted or did not interact with these marginal sprinters became a process of testing, or validating, cultural membership. These tests were sometimes subtle, but on the track, both sprinters and marginal sprinters easily and dramatically saw the test results.

Cultural Identity

A cultural identity is a label that denotes a social position, occupational title, or social title and acts to represent a unifying cultural focus of a group. The label, such as sprinter, football player, windsurfer, or bodybuilder, refers to an individual as well as a group identity that expresses membership in a cultural group of athletes. These identities encompass any number of group members and are played out (even performed) within the network of social relations that define the culture. For example, football players will interact with other football players, coaches, and trainers within the context of being a football player. A player will also, in a way, interact with himself in relation to how well he is playing or performing the identity of a football player, and the player will interact with the opposing team during practice and games. The relationships within the identity are fluid and take on different forms—during practice, a teammate may well be part of the opposing team, whereas in game situations the same player will become a teammate.

Each identity will have a set of rules or roles that will guide or determine appropriate behavior. To act like a bodybuilder, one needs to be a bodybuilder or know a lot about bodybuilding. Even then, certain requisites are necessary to claim membership in the culture of bodybuilders. In sport, certain physical requirements are necessary, such as finely crafted muscle formations for bodybuilders or a preponderance of fast-twitch muscle fiber for sprinters. Beyond the physical requirements, one must also be familiar with perceptions of group members. For example, one must know how the group defines a good bodybuilder. To claim this identity, one must have familiarity or even intimacy with the knowledge of that identity (the "stuff" one needed to know to assume that identity) and must know how to use that knowledge in social or performance interaction. As a football player, I needed to know a variety of things—routes to run on pass patterns, blocking patterns, and catching techniques—but I also needed to understand attitudes and perceptions that were not so mechanical or diagrammatic. This *mentalistic* or *behavioral* knowledge consisted of how a football player was to act in a game, in the locker room, and off the field in interaction with other players and nonplayers. Thus, identity was a constellation of behaviors, actions, perceptions, and even physical attributes that football players would recognize in other players as a reflection of themselves. This constellation of features was coded in recurrent social messages that flew back and forth between players who were cultural members.

Cultural Reality

Traditional definitions of culture stressed a homogeneous view of cultural reality. As an example Malinowski represented a Trobriand reality that all islanders possessed and participated in. Although early ethnographers were cobbling together perspectives of cultural life from different informants, in the end, cultural reality was given to be a single reality. Postmodernists like George Marcus argue that there is no homogeneous cultural reality, that in effect ethnography must pursue a multisited method—doing fieldwork in a variety of settings, not just a track or a baseball field, to get at the wideranging network of forces that mold and shape cultures.

Contemporary ethnography takes into account the different "voices" being recruited to describe their cultural reality (for a discussion on voice in writing ethnography, see chapter 6). Even within relatively small, homogeneous populations such as a small island tribe or a sprint team, cultural members may posit highly dissimilar opinions of what cultural reality looks like. I am sure that sprinters posited several differing views of cultural reality, related to ability, personality, background, and so on. In my work on sprinters (1991, 1995), this cultural reality was a part of what I referred to as the "identity" of a sprinter. Each of the sprinters perceived the culture of sprinters similarly (i.e., common boundaries, knowledge, etc.), yet variations between these perceptions did exist. Referring back to our earlier discussion on the goal of ethnography—to figure out what is in a person's head—these differing representations of cultural reality did not break up or divide what all of us thought to be a culture of sprinters; in fact, cultural variation is important to expanding cultural knowledge. The more variation, to a point, the more knowledge becomes accessible to the cultural members.

Ethnographers today are also keen to discern the cultural features attached to informants, such as gender, age, and status. These features act to provide differential access to power, generate different areas of interest to defend, and produce differing interpretations of cultural reality in terms of behavior, practices, and institutions. In a study of windsurfing (see chapter 8 for a further discussion of the research), Belinda Wheaton (1997) wrote about a male-oriented culture that had many more males (specifically white) than females.

She noted that her experiences in this culture were somewhat shaped by her gender, her status as an experienced windsurfer, and her accessibility to information. In Griffin's (1998) work on lesbian athletes, the cultural reality of female athletes was sharply influenced by the issue of the homosexuality of athletes and coaches; how an athlete saw friendship, competition, and social relations was centered on sexual preference.

The content and applicability of this notion of cultural reality can also be a function of the ethnographer's understanding of the ethnographic experience and can be related to the idea that a reality exists independent of the ethnographer and can be reproduced by the ethnographer, given that the ethnographer's cultural background influences his or her interpretation of that culture's reality. This idea will be covered more in depth in chapters 6 and 9.

Yet, when all is said and done, there seems to be a reality or a shared understanding that encompasses the population of cultural members. Athletes see their world in a focused way—frequent competitions during the competitive seasons are replaced by longer periods of training with no competition in the off-seasons. Workouts are structured similarly and often repeated depending on the season. If the athlete is in school, classes fill available time. Individual variation may occur within areas of the life of team members or other athletes in that sport, but most athletes would paint their reality in similar ways. In some ways the reality is shared; in other ways the reality is the same.

A Culture for Any Season

If anything of consequence has been gained by this exploration and adaptation of the culture concept, I hope it has been that people intuitively recognize what a culture is and have the almost universal ability to apply that concept to individual groups. Cultural researchers grapple with how to apply a traditional concept to a world far different from the world in which the concept originated. That should not be a surprise. One of the most fundamental features of culture is that it is constantly changing in its expression as the physical environment (once the determining feature of culture) and the cultural environment change. The controversy over retaining or discarding the concept calls for researchers to cull through the current perceptions of culture and identify one that makes the most sense in a fractured global order.

In a sense the culture concept has broadened, operating to include traditional features such as ethnicity, language, and race (all at one time synonymous with culture), which are once again becoming attractive as Western civilization homogenizes human diversity or creates monolithic perceptions of culture through television and the Internet. In the process of postcolonialism and the erasing of geographical boundaries and distinctness flavored by semi-isolation, the culture concept now includes features such as lifestyle, generations, gender, athletes, and sport.

In my work on recreational basketball 15 years ago, players perceived two distinct styles of play, "black" and "white." Black style was a perception of both those who claimed it as their own style and those who found fault with what they perceived as its inherent message of personalized public relations. In other words, black style became more than a description of race. The label became an identifier that might or might not include race but embraced a constellation of features such as a player's urban background, the winnowing of talent in the crucible of the schoolyards and playgrounds, an arrogance, and an electricity of style in the face of a humility of "team." White style focused on a sense of methodical workmanship, a joy in the outcome more than the play, a genesis of style in rural and suburban centers, and perhaps, as some players indicated, an echo of the blue-collar ethic. It is not a stretch to view these styles as cultural expressions of the players, complete with the acknowledgement of such styles by those who claim identity to either.

Concluding Remarks

With this revolution in culture, ethnography has found a far more eclectic and diverse medium to paint its messages of description, explanation, and prediction of human behavior. Certainly a culture of sprinters or windsurfers has boundaries that include or exclude members, a distinct body of cultural knowledge that is accessed through social interaction, and learned shared behavior (or what one needs to know to be a sprinter). Its rites, practices, and customs, as well as its material items, become representations of what resides in the members' heads.

One feature of this contemporary culture concept reflects the transitory and ever-changing nature of the new millennium—these late 20th and 21st century cultures are no longer anchored to a specific location, nor are they lifelong or all encompassing. If I no longer play college football, can I still be considered a member of the culture of the Santa Barbara City College football team? Or, for that matter, college football as a whole? Can Willie Williams, 1956 record holder in the 100-meter sprint, still be considered a sprinter, or does he join another culture, that of former or past sprinters? Is 88-year-old Payton Jordan, a world-class sprinter in the 1930s and now competing in masters' track and field (and age-group record holder in the 100 meters), still a member of the culture of sprinters? This diversity, recognized by many, renders the culture concept powerless in application.

Sprinting through the Iowa Games at age 31, am I still a sprinter?

Although a succinct definition becomes difficult to assign to culture, intracultural variation only reflects the contemporary nature of humanity; it does not undermine the human need to differentiate and explore others. Ethnography was and still is the most sensitive way to measure those cultures and make them come alive for those, both academic and nonacademic, interested in making the different become familiar.

Endnotes

1. For a good lay discussion of the history of "culture," see chapter 2 in Robert Lavenda and Emily Schultz, *Core Concepts in Cultural Anthropology* (Mountain View, California: Mayfield Publishing, 1999).

2. See the film *Trobriand Cricket: A Case Study of Culture Change,* and Sally Ann Ness, "Understanding Cultural Performance: Trobriand Cricket," in *Anthropology, Sport and Culture,* ed. R. Sands (Westport, Connecticut: Bergin and Garvey, 1999).

3. See Christopher Brumann, "Writing for Culture: Why a Successful Concept Should Not Be Discarded," *Current Anthropology* 40 (1999): 1–25. For an up-to-date treatment of the culture concept in cultural research, see Robert Aunger, "Against Idealism: Contra Consensus," *Current Anthropology* 40 (1999): 93–101.

4. See the following for a more detailed look at a cognitive-based concept of culture, complete with the role of K-Structures: F.K. Lehman, "Cognition and Computation," in *Directions in Cognitive Anthropology,* ed. Janet Dougherty (Urbana, Illinois: University of Illinois Press, 1985), J.D. Keller and F.K. Lehman, "Computational Complexity in the Cognitive Modeling of Cosmological Idea," in *Cognitive Aspects of Religious Symbolism,* ed. P. Boyer (Cambridge: Cambridge University Press, 1993), F.K. Lehman, "Essay #14, Notes on Logical Form in an Intensionalist Semantics" in *Cognitive Science Research Notes* (in progress), and F.K. Lehman and R. Sands, "The Nature of Social Identity and Identity Relationships," in *Lectures on Anthropological Theory* (in progress).

Chapter 5

Doing Ethnography

Find out the typical ways of thinking and feeling, corresponding to the institutions and culture of a given community and formulate the results in the most convincing manner.

—Bronislaw Malinowski, *Argonauts of the Western Pacific*

P articipating and observing produces a wide-angle view of cultural behavior. Flowing with the currents of cultural reality, the ethnographer learns and assimilates much. At some point, the fieldworker must turn attention to the individual lives of the people, either to have concepts clarified, to have behavior explained, or to understand the effects of behavior on individuals. For those who come to ethnography from a social science or nonanthropological background, qualitative data-collection techniques revolve around questionnaires and formal interviews. The lived setting of ethnography demands much more immediacy and intimacy. The standardized nature of formalized surveys and questionnaires fail to produce the kinds of data necessary. That is not to say that the more formalized measurements are not useful in fieldwork situations; however, the unique nature of participant observation emphasizes certain channels of data acquisition that are unlikely to be chosen in formalized research situations.

This chapter examines field methods involving interviewing and collection of data from oral or written sources. Important to this process of data acquisition are

- selection of those to interview,
- formal structured and open-ended interviews,
- informal interviews,
- life or oral histories,
- the use of historical sources, and
- collecting cultural myths and legends.

Once the data has been collected, the process of recording culture begins. Methods include

- field notes,
- photography,
- audiotaping, and
- videotaping.

At the heart of any ethnography are the "scratch" notes taken by the ethnographer in everyday field situations. Malinowski was one of the first ethnographers to use photography as a means of supplementing field notes. Modern ethnography employs a variety of tools besides the traditional field notes to help the reader visualize cultural reality. This chapter concludes with a section on the benefits and drawbacks of audiotaping and videotaping culture. The fact that the method of ethnography is a century old (though now carried out with innovative technology) and that controversy continues over the representation and interpretation of culture does not diminish the importance of adequately recording cultural behavior. What good is accessing the cultural reality if the ethnographer cannot properly record it for others to understand?

Who to Interview

Arrival in the field is perhaps the first and only time the ethnographer will be unable to delineate or mark the people or roles that will yield good data. The ethnographer may already have a foot in the door on arrival—a friend or a contact. The ethnographer's arrival may occur without any prior association with cultural members. My work on sprinters was an example of the latter, but I still needed some kind of official permission to commence my fieldwork. I approached the sprint coach in his office and explained my interests. He was intrigued and perhaps somewhat motivated by a chance to publicize his career and philosophy in a venue that was new and foreign to him. His wholehearted blessing paved my way into fieldwork with the sprinters.

The ethnographer establishes initial associations or relationships with those in the culture who control, guide, or influence cultural interaction. In my case the initial association was with Willie, the sprint coach who acted not only to legitimize my fieldwork but also to give an official permission to engage in fieldwork. Many ethnographers and anthropologists have labeled these beginning contacts *gatekeepers.* In sport research, managers, coaches, trainers, and administrators are usually the gatekeepers. Gatekeepers may also be athletes or other related persons who may not have official capacity but because of their leadership or performance wield great influence over the rest of the population.

In Klein's work on bodybuilders, owners of gyms or managers introduced him to cultural members who could provide information. In Belinda Wheaton's work on windsurfers, the informed gatekeepers were the most prominent, experienced, and veteran windsurfers in the small community based around coastal English towns. In Michael Silk's work (1999) on New Zealand television coverage of the 1998 Commonwealth Games, the gatekeepers were producers and directors, former and current, who could have controlled his access to informants but who offered him channels to potential contacts who otherwise might have been reticent to take part in interviews. Identifying gatekeepers is just the first step. Having the association produce feelings of trust and respect that trickle down into the cultural members is just as important as the initial contacts.

Ferreting out informed gatekeepers is a process that can be problematic. Within a population, whether it be a community, a track team, or a football team, there are those who operate on the fringe of the group. These marginal members often offer friendship to the ethnographer, who in the beginning is also marginal. The ethnographer must push beyond these initial associations because the culture at large will sour on the ethnographer if he maintains associations with peripheral members. The cultural members will question the ethnographer's intent or limit the time or information they provide in the process of the fieldwork. Often, the gatekeeper or gatekeepers are not found in the first blush of fieldwork. They may wait to see the direction and personality of the ethnographer before offering their services. As mentioned in chapter 4, during my sprint fieldwork, there were marginal sprinters who at first attended practice religiously. When it became apparent that their skills or abilities did not measure up, their practice attendance became sporadic and then nonexistent. Their stories were just as interesting and telling as those who were exceptional in ability, yet my goal was not to focus on sprinters who failed to measure up athletically, but to chronicle the culture of speed that graced the indoor and outdoor tracks of the University of Illinois.

Reggie was one of those marginal sprinters, more mouth and tale than speed, and his continued presence during my first fall became comical to the rest of the team. He became a butt of jokes. Reggie rarely ran his workouts with those who were not marginal, and he did not figure into the social interaction that took place on and off the track. I quickly discovered that my efforts and workouts were in jeopardy of not being respectable if I ran with Reggie too much. Built in to the culture of speed at Illinois, as almost anywhere, was the need to run with those who could push you to better performances. Working out with Reggie did not provide this need for competition, and it placed in question the desire and motivation of those who did. In a way, the ethnographer must be pragmatic in choosing gatekeepers or informants. In the beginning stages of fieldwork, the ethnographer must constantly weigh the benefits and disadvantages of the associations that populate social intercourse; patience and the ability to calculate the worth of informants are valuable commodities in fieldwork.

Where to go from there in relation to interviewing depends on the skill and ability of the ethnographer to communicate or vindicate the initial feeling of trust to the larger body of cultural members. Hammersley and Atkinson (1995) identify two categories of potential interviewees—member identified and observer identified. Member-identified interviewees include those who volunteer for interviews or suggest possible interview subjects. Observer-identified interviewees are those who the fieldworker scouts out and marks during participant observation.

The beauty and the beast of ethnography is the flexibility of design. Rooting out sources demands patience and time spent paying dues (see chapter 3 on time spent on research). In fieldwork with small numbers of members, such as the sprinting research or research on the television team, everybody becomes an interviewee. In research involving large numbers of potential subjects, such as football teams or people in bodybuilding gyms or beaches, the choice of those to be interviewed will be influenced by who has already been interviewed or by the interests and hypothesis of the ethnographer.

Interviewing

Ethnographic interviewing takes on the properties of an art form. The fieldworker must apply the brush strokes of timing for certain questions, choose aggressive versus passive direction, determine the amount and kinds of information requested by questions, decide how many subjects to interview at once and whether to interview individuals or groups, choose a location for the interviews, and allow the subject and tenor of the interview to set the pace of information kind and flow.

Interviews are of several types: formal, informal, and life or oral histories. Informal or field interviews are those done on the fly, precipitated by events in the making. Situations arise daily in fieldwork when cultural members offer explanations on cultural behavior or experience or the mechanics of material items. During my sprinting research, one of the 400-meter runners, after blitzing the first 200 meters, faded in the last 200 and ended up last in the heat. But he recorded a personal record. Warming up for my race, I walked over to where he sat on the track, unable to move even 10 minutes after the finish of his race. I asked him why he ran as he did. What was he thinking? Spent, he proceeded to tell me about how he looked at a race and how running the 400 meter was the epitome of what a sprinter was. In that brief five minutes, what he told me was more succinct and from the heart than what I could have received in a two-hour interview. In a situation during my basketball research, I was watching the ongoing game before my team took the court to play the winners. Standing against the wall, I was talking comfortably with one of my soon-to-be teammates. I took this opportunity to broach the topic of black and white style. I struggled to get my question understood, not for lack of my teammate's understanding but more from my inability to find the right words. We turned to watch the action that had heated up on the court. One of the players had broken away and drove around two players, dribbled the ball behind his back, and then dunked it over another. My teammate turned toward me and said, "That is black style, man." After that, for the remainder of the game, he clearly related what made up black style.

More formal, or set, interviews are usually prearranged and involve a set of questions or clusters of questions to be asked. Formal interviews are also done with the express desire to collect oral or life histories. Because of the planning and effort involved for both the ethnographer and the informant, formal interviews can last from hours to days, with segments being staged over several settings. Taping or recording these interviews is recommended, although the ethnographer should also take notes that will supplement the recorded material, not so much for validity but more for nuances and flavor of the interview and other subjective elements. Within a guided interview, the two processes designed to elicit information are the open-ended interview and the structured interview.

Open-Ended and Structured Interviews

Open-ended interviews are by far the easiest to set up but are the most difficult to mine for information. The fieldworker initially sets the tone of the interview, offering a couple of questions to give the informant a direction in which to begin. After a general direction has been set, the informant is then allowed to guide the conversation—and that is what it becomes, a somewhat one-sided conversation in terms of topics and the amount of time

An open-ended interview with Hawaiian surfing legend John Kelley at his home on Diamond Head, Oahu in 1998. Sometimes it is not the question, but the listening.

spent on each topic. The fieldworker keeps his or her involvement to a minimum, rarely interrupting except perhaps to follow up on initial directions given the informant. Open-ended interviews require a large investment of time for both the actual interview and the process of eliciting information from the transcribed tape and/or the typed transcripts of field notes.

Open-ended interviews allow the interview to be conducted over more than one sitting. The keys for any type of semistructured, or informal, interview are to be patient while the informant searches for appropriate segues between topics and, just as important, to be attentive to the subtle nuances of cultural behavior and knowledge that this type of research allows. During my ongoing research with surfers, informants and I will often sit on our boards for an extended time when the swell is infrequent, waiting for a set (a number of waves in succession) to come in. Or we will sit on the beach following a surf session and engage in an open-ended interview. Certain topics will emerge that I will concentrate on at a later date. These occasions allow me to conduct "interviews" on site and lend a certain amount of familiarity to both the surfer-informants and me. While researching football, I used bus trips to and from away games for open-ended interviews. Most of our trips were at least two hours one way, allowing plenty of time to engage informants. Following a discussion on the way to a game, a player would often ponder our conversation during the pregame, game, and postgame periods, and on the return segment of the trip he would qualify a previous response and provide more depth to the information he had already provided.

In a way, subjects are like onions. Layers are peeled away, and the informant reveals not only more of his or her personality but also layers of cultural knowledge. In these opportunities of lengthy, almost free-flowing discussions—and because fieldwork is long term, many such discussions should occur (especially if the population is small)— the layers will be exposed and knowledge will fortuitously come to light. In my work (as discussed in chapter 9), my informants or gatekeepers gladly exposed layer upon layer of themselves and their cultural knowledge. Many times, especially in sport, subjects will exaggerate their ability, performance, or importance to a team. Sloughing layers can easily misrepresent the athlete, but the ethnographer can rely only on what is said to represent what is in the subject's head. As the layers fall, and as the ethnographer accumulates time and lived experience with the subjects, she can more easily spot misrepresentation. Trusted subjects become the staple of second-hand knowledge.

Formal interviews are often culled from the fruits of observation and the information retrieved during the field interviews. Formal interviews differ from the open-ended, free-flowing, mostly one-sided discussions mentioned above. They have a somewhat formal structure, a time is set for the interview, and information is passed and duly recorded by the ethnographer, either as notes or recorded (see a later section in this chapter on audio and video recording in ethnography). There is an atmosphere of give and take— the ethnographer takes what the interviewee gives. In a spoken sense (the ethnographer usually asks permission to take notes or record the session) and an unspoken sense (the subject knows he will be an expert for this period), a formal interview is managed to some degree rather than allowed to occur spontaneously. Some of the formal interview is predicated on establishing a brief or synoptic life history (see the next section for a more in-depth look at life histories). Given the time of the formal interview, even if a set of cluster questions has been identified by the ethnographer before the interview, a good ethnographer will be attentive to information that departs from the format but opens up new vistas to pursue.

Eduardo Archetti's (1997) interesting work on the moralities of Argentinian football involved intermittent ethnographic interviewing of Argentinian football fans (identified as mostly middle-class, middle-aged with some highly educated) during a span of over 10 years. Much of his interviewing was formal and involved in-depth discussions of the symbols and metaphors embedded in the game itself. He attended football matches and met some of his informants during these games. On the other hand Michael Silk's fieldwork on television coverage of the Commonwealth Games produced an entirely different interviewing strategy. Because of the fast-paced, frenetic nature of television, rarely did Silk have the opportunity to engage in lengthy in-depth formal interviews. Instead, he relied mostly on field interviews, proving that life can at times live in a sound bite.

The open-ended interview can often also provide answers to more formalized measurements at the same time. In my fieldwork on basketball style and performance (Sands 1986), which included observation, participation, and a standardized checklist of performance and style, I ended up using a population of 30 players for research purposes. I combined formal and informal techniques in the interviewing stage of my research. I spent between two and four hours (or about two pitchers' worth of beer in Cy's Roost, a campus-town bar near Iowa State University) interviewing each of the 30 subjects on a variety of topics. In the construction of my research design I identified 10 cluster questions that pertained to a player's perception of his playing style, his performance, and the environmental factors that directly or indirectly shaped his particular style. After posing the initial cluster question, I gave the reigns to the player-informant to direct or guide the response. During the same interview, I collected data based on standardized queries of location, sports background in number of sports played, education attained, race, and so forth.

Life History

More in depth than even an open-ended interview is a *life history,* which is a comprehensive picture of an individual's life experience narrated by the individual to the fieldworker. Of all the tools used by the ethnographer, the life history provides the most micro perspective of a culture. The life history also comes with a set of fallibilities, such as the penchant of the informant to exaggerate or lie outright about the events and circumstances involved in his or her life. If the life history taken is of an elderly person, hazy recollection or perhaps no recollection at all casts doubt on the accuracy of the account. Another conceptual limitation of a life history is the slim possibility of finding an informant who can claim to be a representative of an entire culture. Thus, a life history would be unable to stand in as a truly representative perspective of cultural reality, over time or space.

Despite these shortcomings, a life history can provide an extremely rich view of a culture and the informant's interpretation of culture. Perhaps more important, a life history can provide a unique diachronic perspective of the changing nature of culture and cultural behavior. Early on, Boas rejected the use of life histories as unreliable, but a student of Boas, Paul Radin (1963), suggested that such a tool could provide a primer on the "workings of the mind." His life history of a Winnebago Indian deeply involved in the Wisconsin tribe's Peyote Cult shed valuable light on the nature of visions and feelings the drug induced and the cultural meanings of such altered states.

During my tenure as an archaeologist-ethnographer with Los Padres National Forest in Santa Barbara County, California, I continued a program of taking life histories of Forest personnel to build an archive of Forest history. This collective oral history was invaluable in recreating a richly textured look at the lifestyles that were otherwise known only by grainy black-and-white photographs. When several life histories are taken, a picture emerges of shared experience providing a range of lifestyle and variation of cultural values.

In my track research (Sands 1991 and 1995), the population size of the sprinting team allowed me to take life histories of all sprinters and coaches. Since the sprinters' ages ranged from 18 to 22, the life histories were all fairly abbreviated and offered similarly framed stories of competition. Using those histories, I could easily separate out life changes and cycles each of the sprinters had gone through in their competitive careers. This gave me a more rounded representation of the factors that motivate and define elite sprinters. I also had the opportunity to elicit the life history of the sprinting coach, Willie Williams, world-record holder in the 100 meters from 1956 to 1960. His life history afforded me an in-depth comparative look at how factors such as environment, perception of identity and performance, background, and so on have changed or stayed the same over the span of the three generations of Willie's life. It also afforded me a comparison of Willie then and the sprinters I interviewed 10 years ago.

Anne Bolin's (1997) work on competitive bodybuilding was based on case studies of 22 athletes. Somewhat different from the comprehensive, full-length life history, the case study acts as an explanatory tool in describing and presenting cultural reality. Life histories are an important element of a case study, especially in understanding the cultural and social forces that have influenced or shaped the experience of the individual. Case studies are more useful as comparative units, however, than as looks at culture change.

Myths as Texts

Texts are usually assigned to written or oral stories, myths, plays, sayings, or any other transcriptions of everyday conversations. In sport, myths are powerful shapers of cultural tradition and act to solidify cultural truths. A *cultural truth* is a tenet or precept that lies at the heart of what defines a culture to its members. These myths can be analogized to legends, half-truths, or stories taken from actual events or occurrences offered by those interviewed or passed on during the course of interaction in fieldwork. Either observed or passed on from another, the informant's telling of the myth acts as tradition would, either defining or redefining cultural boundaries to those in the culture and those outside.

Collecting these texts requires the investment of time and effort because their telling is not something an ethnographer can elicit in an interview. Most of these texts are uncovered during fieldwork, subject to an occasion or event that creates a context for the story or myth to be expressed. In preliterate non-Western cultures, these "texts" are oral stories passed down partially as entertainment but also for educational purposes. Over three years of fieldwork with the sprinters, I heard Willie's world-record story several times. We never tired of hearing Willie recount his 1956 world-record 100-meter performance set in the Olympic stadium in Berlin, on the same track and lane that Jesse Owens had run when setting the world record during the 1936 Olympics. In each telling of his story, Willie changed the story line to fit the personalities of the sprinters present, and the story had a different effect on veterans and newcomers alike.

Major performances by those sprinters also became mythlike, selected for their achievement and meaning in the culture. Willie would invariably bring up the story of Lee when talking to us about desire and motivation. Lee was a nationally ranked 400-meter sprinter who ran for two of the three years that I did my research. Willie built him up as one who could rise above physical pain and perform at levels beyond what most of the sprinters could achieve. Lee's personality was shaped in Willie's story of how Lee had run a personal record and placed in the 400 meters at the Big Ten Championships. Lee had vomited before and after the race, and with wobbly legs, less than 45 minutes later, had run the anchor leg on the victorious 4×400-meter relay. Willie never tired of telling this story for its effect on the sprinters who ran during and after Lee's career.

Stellar performances relayed to us by coaches and other players during my football research acted as means of localizing to the players the important features of the culture, just as Willie's stories provided cultural meaning to the sprinters. In my first season of playing, Jarrod was the quarterback and eventual all-conference MVP. He badly sprained his ankle two days before a pivotal game. With two days of drugs, daily icings, whirlpools, and massages, and two steel ankle braces, Jarrod played his best game of the year. I wrote about that performance because it relayed one of the cultural truths about football, the ability to play in pain. In a sense, I, as the ethnographer, was not only collecting the text but also acting as a member of the population, retelling the story as a means of highlighting cultural reality to other players.

Most similar to the "texts" of non-Western culture may be myths and legends of surfing. Until recently, surfing myths recounted performances without the "Westernized" need to time, record, or chart performance. The actual images of the first big waves ridden at Waimea in 1957 are one or two black-and-white photographs. But the myth of that day of big-wave riding is constructed around the stories collected from those present and those who carried the story from the initial tellers. With no documentation, surfers live to pass on stories of big-wave days, or storm-ridden surf, or perfect barrels that reinforce the foundations of surfing—bravery, courage, and manhood. In an ironic twist, with surfing a solitary form of performance, surfers who are not present can only grasp a big or perfect day through the recollections of that lone surfer. Surfing is then caught between myths that immortalize and reinforce surf culture and the sense of going alone against or as a communion with nature (Sands 1999d). Statements from surf informants that began with, "Dude, you had to be there," alerted the listener to another myth or nugget of surf tradition. As a fieldworker, I accessed these myths or stories in daily interaction, but particular climactic and environmental conditions were required to produce such a story.

Historical Sources

The history of a culture can cast understanding on contemporary cultural behavior. Using such sources as a guide to contemporary cultures can expose layers of detail about cultural traditions that still act to shape behavior, or highlight the values or truths that have changed and perhaps explain the change. Anthropologists use libraries and historical archives that house written records of the past. Other sources are religious institutions such as

The basement of the Bishop museum in Honolulu. In here, wearing white gloves, I handled 250-year-old originals of Captain Cook's diary in which he wrote about seeing Hawaiians surf for the first time. Ethnography concerns the dead as well as the living.

the Catholic Church or the Mormon genealogical center in Salt Lake City. For sports, Halls of Fame represent such institutions. Many exist, from Cooperstown and Canton to surfing museums located in Oceanside, California, and Halewia on the North Shore of Oahu. Volumes exist on sport performances, and sport encyclopedias give general accounts of the history of sports.

Another rich source of historical antecedents for a culture are the living people of a culture. Folded within the many layers of a life history are potential sources for these antecedents, found in stories relayed by parents and grandparents and recovered through old diaries and family memorabilia. An enterprising mother and other relatives with an exhaustive scrapbook of photographs, newspaper articles, and the like cataloged Willie's brilliant career for him. Each of the sprinters had his own scrapbook of memories, cataloging his performances. When I read these written museums, I came away with an understanding of the sprinters' past careers without having been there. Indeed, my three years of fieldwork produced a scrap-book of meets and times, albeit less grand and impressive but still yielding the flavor of my fieldwork. No less grand in scope was the cataloging done by the football players of their career highlights. All had scrapbooks, and many produced their own 30- or 60-minute videos, a sort of "best hits" from their high school careers. One memorable tape belonged to Torlando Bolden. "Touchdown" Torlando's tape was a slick and impressive bit of video showmanship that highlighted his tremendous athletic ability on the football field and basketball court of Santa Barbara High School. No one who saw the tape, and that included the entire college football team, went away without shaking his head in admiration for Bolden's talents and the way they were put together on tape. In today's world, historical texts appear less frequently on paper. Instead, a history will be recorded in images on a number of different media, including disc, video, and media we have yet to invent. Still, even if the word is exchanged for a digital image, these third-millennium sources will produce the same rich historical source of cultural behavior.

Recording Culture

To the ethnographer, the first step in the production of an ethnographic text is the recording of field observations, experiences, and interviews on paper, audiotape, or videotape. Common sense dictates that written field notes be legible, sequenced, and dated. Recorded sound and images must be audible and visible. After all the time spent in the field, it is ironic that the actual text is created in an office or home, far from the cultural members and field experiences of the ethnographer. Relying on poorly executed field data can seriously undermine the success of the ethnographic text.

Field Notes

Field notes have always been the symbol of an ethnographer. A fieldworker with pen and notebook in hand observing a ritual or talking to a village chief has been the stereotypical image of ethnography for decades. For as much as technology has changed and introduced modern methods of re-cording, written field notes remain the staple method for taking what the fieldworker sees and experiences and translating those representations, images, and words into a record that can be accessed by others at a later time. Field notes, when written up, include "scratch notes," daily logs, hurried scribbles on random pieces of paper (or material that passes as paper) with descriptions about specific events or occurrences.

Accurately recording a culture requires an enormous amount of "scratch notes" (Sanjek 1990, 95–99) and an almost magical touch to keep all the notes in some semblance of order. Considering that notes come in all shapes, sizes, and materials, this task challenges even the most meticulous and orderly person. Ideally, these scratch notes should be written up daily to maintain the context and memory of what was observed or felt. I have jotted down cultural observations on whatever was available. Sometimes the situation demanded ingenuity; I have used a tissue, a football program, the back of a competitor's entry number, even pieces of used athletic tape. The most dire situation demanded that I drag out pieces of yellowed paper that probably predated parchment from underneath the seats of my old 1977 Mazda RX-7 in the Santa Barbara City College Stadium parking lot. I have used pen, pencil, highlighters, and even charcoal to record notes. In one recent instance, in my surfing research, I used zinc oxide to record a name and phone number of a potential informant. Ethnography is the mother of invention.

The invention of the laptop computer has eased the process of note recording, even note taking, yet even that instrument is many times impractical, and notes are made with paper and pen. Considerable time is required daily to turn these scratch notes into a valuable commodity. Reality intrudes, however, and the fieldworker must often write up field notes that are backlogged and removed by time from the actual recording. It is then imperative that the ethnographer has taken field notes that present an accurate representation of what occurred or was experienced.

During my research on sprinters and football players, I was often up late at night writing up my field notes. My day was crammed with teaching, grading, and taking classes. During my track research I was taking doctoral classes at the University of Illinois and bartending to supplement my teaching assistantship. For the football fieldwork, I had to take classes at Santa Barbara City College to be eligible to play. I was also teaching classes at the college. Late in the evening was the only time I had available to attend to my field notes. Sore muscles or the discomfort of injury was a constant companion at my keyboard as I fed scribblings, which at midnight became an almost indescribable code, into my computer.

Personal journals or diaries, though not considered field notes, act to orient the ethnographer to daily events and provide a channel to ease or disseminate the cultural dissonance felt by the ethnographer during fieldwork. Malinowski's diary, as discussed earlier, opened up his personality to later anthropologists and radically changed the way ethnographers were perceived by the outside world. Granted, most diaries or journals never see the light of day, and privacy in a journal's written word tends to be the only personal space granted to an ethnographer during the all-consuming process of fieldwork. Still, as a tool for supplementing field notes, these kinds of confessionals can serve more than one master.

The Audio and Visual of Ethnography

With progress come benefits and disadvantages. Ethnography is no exception. Tape recording is an obvious aid to recording culture. Tapes provide an accurate record of what has been said by whom during interviews and are useful for recording cultural events or just normal, day-to-day activities. For the next generation of ethnographers, a technology may allow the transfer of sound into text. Unfortunately, that technology is in its infancy, and the software for it is still somewhat cumbersome. For the rest of us, the technology is still in the womb. Tape recording presents the ethnographer with a formidable task—each hour of tape requires at least three hours of transcribing and possibly more if there are multiple voices. One simply hopes conditions were good enough to make voices intelligible. State-of-the-art equipment is not always available to the starving doctoral student, or even to the accomplished ethnographer. Yet whenever possible, the use of devices such as quality lapel microphones will make the experience of transcription a passable chore.

That is not to mention the tedium of tracking a conversation or several conversations through headphones. I taped the radio broadcast of the last game of my second football season for use in my ethnography of college football culture and remember spending a solid week, four to five hours a session, on the transcription. When it was completed, I felt as if I had played the game again.

Visual images, whether photographs, film, or the more commonly used video, can easily retain more detail than scratch notes. The rigors and difficulty of capturing movement, the sequencing of ritual, or even noting the roles involved in a celebration can be partially alleviated through the use of visual technology. Recalling an event or witnessing a behavior can be a difficult process when working from such tools as scratch notes. But memory is served by visually reviewing a photograph, a video, or a film clip. During my fieldwork, I took rolls of film and saved all the game tapes for my football research. More than helping me recall a specific event or play, the film acted to present me with the feeling of the experience while I was working to recapture cultural reality. To supplement field notes, I ended up creating a visual field notebook with developed film and an archival repository of video. Pictures of certain environments many times helped release memories stored away after fieldwork. In my sprinting research, I have many photographs of the "Hill" (discussed earlier in chapter 4). For many of us that hill became a landmark for defining who did and who did not have the necessary heart to be included in our small group. The messages that can be taken from those images are worth many words. On the other hand, film and video can only provide a partial representation of that culture. The objectivity assigned to film or video is predicated on the fieldworker's selection of events and situations to capture on film and his or her decisions about which ones provide the most detail or information.

Recently, I was hired as a cultural consultant (see chapter 10 on business ethnography) by an advertising firm to provide expert testimony to support their ad campaign for a fantasy-sport Web page. After several conference phone calls, they were ready to get me on tape answering their questions. They flew a professional video recorder and soundman into Ventura, California, to record the testimony. It took them 90 minutes to turn my kitchen into a Hollywood set. We then taped for two and a half hours while I was hooked up by a phone jack to the ad team back in Boston. The edited tape was slick and professional, and although the reality of the experience was edited, I was left wishing my ethnographic projects could have the same power and feel.

Beyond observation and participation, an ethnographer must rely on cultural members and their traditions and histories to complete his or her representation of cultural reality. Letting the cultural members—and what they have written or passed down—help construct this cultural reality is dependent on interviewing, collecting life or oral histories, and listening to their myths and legends. In many cases, structured or semistructured interviews and historical research allow a carefully planned translation of data that will produce a clear and concise record. But recording culture also requires the ethnographer to spend countless hours taking field notes as behavior swirls around, and occasionally through, him or her. Experience and observation of events or situations often happen in a blink of an eye. The fieldworker must be able to capture a team prayer or a fight between players on a hot practice field or the screamed words of a frustrated coach on paper, or on something that passes as paper. Ethnography is a method that not only uses a multitude of data-gathering techniques but also employs several techniques in recording the data for analysis and ultimately providing a text (as we shall see in the next chapter). If there is one image that has been constant throughout the history of ethnography, it is the intrepid fieldworker scribbling away, trying to capture the last bit of cultural reality while being slowly lowered into a pot of boiling water.

Chapter 6

Analyzing and Writing Ethnography

The final goal which the ethnographer should never lose sight . . . to grasp the native's point of view, his relation to life, to realize his vision of his world.

—Bronislaw Malinowski, *Argonauts of the Western Pacific*

O nce fieldwork is completed (and to many, it is never truly completed), the data and the text will take different forms. Upon completion of my football research, I had several large notebooks full of field notes and interviews, 10 tapes full of interviews, many rolls of film and videotapes, a box full of newspaper stories and clippings, and a brain full of memories. The research was such a powerful and at times unsettling experience for me that it literally took months before I was able to begin translating the data into ethnography. Ethnography has its difficulties; at every turn, the fieldworker must face a new set of logistical, ethical, and even mechanical problems. But if there is one overwhelming task in the process, it is sitting alone laboriously turning scraps of paper and words into a coherent picture of another culture. To make matters more complex, no set procedure marks the path toward completion of a successful ethnography.

One redeeming quality and possible motivation to march through the process is that the data gathered represents in all likelihood the most in-depth look at the culture to date. The research leading to ethnography represents progress in knowledge dissemination. In other words, the fieldworker's research is the definitive word at that time. Even if other work has been done on that culture before the fieldwork, the ethnographer's research adds vital and informative analysis that others will read and refer to. To add more pressure, the fieldwork and ethnography must be done in a professional and understandable manner if the work is to advance knowledge. To start that process, the fieldworker must differentiate between qualitative and quantitative data and understand how both can be useful in ethnography.

This chapter describes the different types of data used in ethnography. Data collection is just the first step in writing culture. The presentation of the culture in the text and the assumptions about what that cultural reality represents vary widely. This chapter will explore the various theoretical positions regarding ethnography and the often bitter debate that surrounds ethnography in many of the social sciences. Finally, the kind of voice used by the ethnographer in writing culture is examined, and examples in sport research and popular culture are given.

This chapter will look at

- kinds of ethnographic data: qualitative and quantitative;
- theoretical positions: interpretivism; postmodernism, positivism;
- reflexivity and the use of narrative; and
- writing culture: voice.

Ethnographic Data

Most ethnographic data takes the form of qualitative data: descriptive field notes, informant and fieldwork narratives, myths and stories provided by the experience. This must be the case. If the majority of data took quantitative form, the uniqueness and power of the ethnographic method would be diluted. But because ethnography is a method of many research strategies, the use of quantitative methods can be useful as a means of describing or defining the population. Qualitative data will usually fall into three general categories: *quotations* from informants in the form of interviews, narratives, and stories; the *experiences* as presented in narratives and interpretations of the fieldworker, concerning both the fieldworker's experiences and those of the cultural members; and *observations* and *descriptions* of cultural lifeways. One prominent method of making sense of this morass of information is searching for themes or regularities in the data. It is not surprising that once an ethnographer becomes involved in analyzing the results of fieldwork, many of these themes will jump out. In the past, ethnographers manually searched through notes to discover or uncover these themes. Today, the electronic age is making its presence known even in ethnography. Software packages can much more effectively and quickly scan data than can the naked eye.

Scanning data provides a measure of theme frequency and a measure of the many topics researched, enabling the ethnographer to isolate concepts across the breadth of the fieldwork and allowing surrounding context to be factored into developing themes that are more inclusive. For example, in the two-plus years I have spent in participant observation of surfers, I have generated numerous field-note entries and typed them into individual files on my computer. By using software packages, I am able to isolate entries, sections, or blocs of data that dealt with specific topics. Perhaps, during my analysis, I wanted to develop an understanding of how wave heights translate into a heightened surfing experience. By scanning my entire body of notes, using features similar to a search or find tool on your computer's word-processing program but coded for larger, more developed entries such as themes or concepts, I can isolate sections of text that deal specifically with wave height and experience. This reduces the time spent hunting for mentions of wave height in the context of big-wave riding.

The success of such a method relies heavily on careful and intelligent arrangement of data, the sum of the research experience, and proper coding of the software so that it can scan and identify the themes.

In much ethnography, quantitative data is used to supplement participant observation. Surveys and questionnaires are the tools most frequently used to elicit quantifiable data. In my work on basketball style and performance (Sands 1986), I sorted my pool of players by several indices, such as race, parental background, urban versus suburban versus rural geographical location, number of years of organized basketball experience, and so on. This approach allowed me to flesh out the defining features of the population and gave me numerical data to assist in testing my hypothesis. Alan Klein distributed questionnaires to ball players and weightlifters, asking them about features or aspects of their culture that would aid in defining cultural behavior and cultural boundaries.

In essence, quantification of data in a predominantly qualitative methodology can be useful in defining a cultural population and the behavioral features that are central to that culture. After the numbers have been counted and queries tabulated, the many different methods used in ethnography produce a representation of cultural reality.

Theoretical Underpinnings of Ethnography

As in any review of theoretical positions in social sciences, the exclusiveness of a position is not entirely compartmentalized as an either-or situation. The labels *interpretivism, postmodernism,* and *positivism* can and do act as lightning rods for both theory and method. In reality, however, the labels rarely act to segment all ethnographers into neat compartments.

Instead, one can visualize a continuum of method and theory that extends from positivism (incorporating realist ethnography) to postmodernism. Ethnographers will choose perspective and methods that best suit the situation and the overall view of specific and general cultural realities.

Because of the brevity of the following section, I have simplified matters by setting up a somewhat artificial categorization of the distinction between interpretivism, postmodernism, and positivism. The reader can then easily track the fundamental differences between the positions.

To be honest with the reader, my view of this ongoing debate in anthropology and the similar debate in many other social sciences, traditional and newly emerging, will color the following discussion. As will be highlighted, differences between the three views of presenting the world revolve around several arguments: axes of science and objectivity versus a nonscience and subjectivity, a hegemonic casting of science as a dominant voice versus the equalization of ethnographer and subject, local knowledge versus scientific knowledge, culture as unique versus culture as driven by social need, reflexivity leading to a polyphonic text versus narrative and reflexivity merging into lived reality. Let there be no mistake, on the extremes of this divisive debate is acrimony and vitriolic rhetoric, and at the center of this widening chasm is the wonder about whether the study of culture and behavior is now, or ever really was, a science. Those on the one extreme call for completely revamping the nature of fieldwork and what it means. Many others refuse to discard a century of tradition entirely but acknowledge the rapidly changing world order and the place in that modern fluidity for the ethnographer. Still others struggle mightily with the notion of science and objectivity: is it possible or even necessary to the understanding of this new world order?

From the following discussion, even as I construct somewhat loaded categorizations for ease of understanding, I recognize that some postmodernists struggle with the place of science and objectivity in their enterprise, instead of merely casting them to the wind of antiscientism. Indeed, there are many, like these spotted postmodernists, who rail against the use of an empirical positivism in a human-driven world complete with personalities, not atoms. In my work, postmodern methodology is married with a sense of humanistic positivism that creates a notion of a culture and identity of specific sport and athletes that can be compared with other sport cultures and nonsport cultures in terms of attribution and boundary distinction. Wheaton sees her work as falling between a postpositivism and postmodernism, illuminating the multiplicity of voices and realities of a windsurfing culture in relation to power (i.e., female versus men) but acknowledging and describing the shared values and behaviors as well.

Perhaps, as the discussion closes and I situate these differing views in the endeavor of sport studies, it will come clear to you, the reader, that in a fieldwork reality, the basic premise of any ethnography is to orient the audience to a possibly different, if not foreign, lifestyle; to explain the role and experience of the ethnographer in relaying this lifestyle; and to heighten the ability of the audience, the ethnographer, and those written about to understand one another and themselves at least a little better. If that can be accomplished, then labels defining discrete orientations become superfluous.

The qualitative nature of field data (through participant observation, interviews, life histories, etc.) gathers only certain kinds of data and, perhaps more important, supports certain kinds of analyses. An area of concern in ethnography addresses what the data represent or mean and whose cultural reality is represented in the final text—the cultural members', the ethnographer's, or a mixed, negotiated reality created with the addition of the ethnographer. As first discussed in chapter 2, ethnography is caught in a vise of radical viewpoints concerning what actually is denoted by the ethnographic text and what use it may have in today's world. It is safe to assume that what represented the traditional methods and outcomes of ethnography no longer exist. Casting off the shackles of an empirical positivism, the underlying focus of what ethnography represents now turns on the role of the ethnographer as observer, participant, and interpreter. No longer detached, the ethnographer becomes part of the equation.

The next section is concerned with the meaning of the ethnographic representation and what can be done with it. To address this concern, three competing ethnographic orientations must be explained—interpretivism, postmodernism, and positivism. Following that, the question of whose culture is being represented in the ethnographic text is answered by looking at the voice of the text. The production of the written text has become as problematic as the debate between science and humanism in the social sciences.

Interpretivism

There seem to be several camps of thought on the preceding questions that spin on a larger view of the interplay between generalized human behavior and culturally specific behavior. The first theoretical orientation, interpretivism, has a storied history. Clifford Geertz is perhaps the best-known person connected with this movement, which posits that every culture is unique and beyond adaptations to the environment that may produce similarity between cultures. Each culture lays claims to its own worldviews, morals, values, and so on. What make up a culture are symbols (see a discussion of culture in chapter 4). The uniqueness of the symbols can be seen through the expression of social behavior. All social interaction therefore is symbolic, and meaning is derived from how these symbols are constructed and put to use. This idea of the meaning of symbols derived from interaction was first proposed by sociologist George Herbert Mead and has been lately championed by Norman Denzin, among others.

For the interpretive ethnographer in quest of cultural meanings, participants involved in the interactions that produce meaning cannot relay how they know the meaning of the behavior, but they can consistently act in ways that others can understand in that interaction and culture. The ethnographer is not after a holistic view of how the individual cultural components fit together and ultimately explain the culture. Rather, the goal is to take an element and show how it relates to other elements in the same system. The interpretation of cultures is trying to understand a culture's way of life (or what I label *cultural reality)* as members of the culture understand it. Ironically, as Malinowski once put it, and interpretists such as Geertz echo, ethnography is an attempt at seeing culture through the "eyes of the native"—and to Geertz, figuring out "what the devil they think they are up to" (Geertz 1983, 58).

To lay claim that one can then proceed to search for generalized explanations of human behavior from any single interpretive view is not applicable to such unique entities as culture. Many features that interact in complex and unpredictable ways form a culture. Attempting to use this view for comparison with other cultures is difficult to say the least. To interpretists, the best that ethnography can give is an understanding of the unique elements of each way of life.

Postmodernism

Postmodernism, a recent phenomenon in academia and social sciences, has created an acrimonious debate within disciplines and across disciplines of traditional social sciences and in emerging fields of studies. Postmodern thought penetrated anthropology in the 1980s with work by George Marcus, Michael Fisher, and James Clifford and sociology with writings by Norman Denzin.[1] Key to this penetration in social sciences was a challenge to normative science and its objectivity, its use of traditional means of establishing authority, and its dubious use of such terms as validity and reliability. Discarding an objective epistemology (knowledge acquisition) and quantitative methodology for hypothesis verification, the postmodernists replaced the central feature of positivism—the accumulation of knowledge—with a position that knowledge is relative and context based.

John van Maanen identifies four "realist tales," or styles (read traditional) (from Richardson 2000, 7):

- Experiential author (ity)—the author exists in the preface to establish authority credentials ("I was there").
- Documentary style—numerous concrete details that represent a typical cultural pattern, individual, or behavior.
- Cultural member's point of view—use of extensive quotations of explanations, semantics, syntax, and so on.
- Interpretive omnipotence—the ethnographer is able to divine the reality of the culture.

To the postmodern ethnographer, each of these "tales" relies heavily on the accumulation of knowledge through unlived experience—that is, knowledge and resultant reality based on information and data (not a favorite label of a postmodernist) extracted from artificial cultural situations and presented as if a higher authority is able to "see" what the cultural members cannot. You can see where van Maanen's concept of authority and the designation of omnipotence come from. It is ironic that in this struggle of ethnographic representation, science has now taken on the qualities of a discarded deity, whereas the drive for the scientific revolution of the 17th and 18th century was to disassociate God from a naturalistic science.

For many, such as Denzin and Marcus, the leading proponents of postmodernism, their chosen field of study is not science. Indeed, at this point in the paradigmatic struggle, there is not a chance that either can be confused as the other. But what exactly defines postmodernism? Postmodernism is a catch-all label referring to many things: movement in the arts, new forms of social theory, the demise of colonialism since World War II, cultural life under late capitalism, and current life in a "mass-mediated" world in which the symbol for reality has replaced reality (Denzin 1997, 263). To those who would refer to themselves as postmodern ethnographers, their methodology is not really "postmodern" but more of a postmodern project, defined by those features that define postmodernism.

It has been two decades since anthropologists and sociologists together and separately began to promote a critique without a replacement for classical and interpretive ethnography. Not to get too bogged down in its intricacies, postmodernism looks at the changing world in response to a reordering and reconfiguring of what used to be the traditional colonial, or European and American—before and during the Vietnam War—world order. With the demise of colonialism and the end of the Vietnam War, a radical shift, and sometimes birth, of national and cultural identities has occurred. To postmodernists, it just so happens that traditional and recent ethnography was done in response to this old world order. The early classical ethnography, as touched on in the introduction, was either done for the colonial administrators or used by them to help understand the peoples and cultures being administered to.

The postmodern world is nothing like the world of 20 or 30 years ago. To the postmodernists, ethnography has changed as well, in both its method and its outcome. Currently, postmodernism (depending on who you read) is in either a Fifth or Sixth Movement (sociologists Denzin and Lincoln 1998, Denzin 1997) or in a "post" postmodern phase (anthropologist Marcus 1999). Differing fields claim a postmodern ethnography is exorcising positivism from ethnography because it embodies the "conservative practices of the traditional, hegemonic ethnographic order" (Denzin 1997, 251). Implicit and fundamental is the belief that science is by its nature hegemonic and complete with a value structure that often excludes or distorts the perspectives of the disenfranchised—minorities, women, the poor and powerless. Indeed, science is a tool of a long-engendered capitalist movement, and postmodern ethnographers work to undermine this academic authority by raising public and private consciousness, isolating core values, and using local knowledge systems.

In discarding science, postmodernists like Denzin and Lincoln choose to circumvent epistemology and instead use ethnography to raise social awareness and strike back against a capitalistic hegemonic social order, "a radical democratic social practice" (Denzin 1997, 287). In essence, it has become a public journalism: "It makes readers, actors and participants, not spectators, in the public dramas that define meaningful life . . ." (Denzin 1997, 281). In a less venomous position, yet with the same perspective as Denzin, Marcus sees a postmodern ethnography as equalizing the unequal power relations between the ethnographer and cultural member representing the same hegemonic social order.

As in any academic debate involving paradigms or theory, the polar opposites only define the extremes. Some find salvation in attempting to marry seemingly dissonant perspectives and methods. The British Cultural Studies movement, as exemplified by Wheaton, although driven by the winds of postmodernism, cannot be totally characterized as antiscientism. Another movement entails ethnographic writing while avoiding theoretical issues but building on traditional anthropological research methods. Others, like Durrenburger (see later), opt for a science that describes and explains, even predicts, but has lost most of the rigidity of an empirical science, which Denzin has deemed "colonial." Still others acknowledge the rapidly changing world and the "evils" of colonialism and American imperialism, but still quest for a measure of positivism. Even the postmodernists admit that the last 20 years has been spent trying to replace a tradition with a paradigm that has yet to emerge as the new way to "see the world."

What has emerged, however, is a revolution in method, led by a radical shift in the role and position of the ethnographer. With a positivistic methodology set adrift, postmodern ethnography is driven by narrative. This method can be described as a pair of relationships: the use of dialogue between ethnographer and cultural member and, in the text, between ethnographer and the cultural member the ethnographer was before initiating fieldwork. These relationships are then played out through reflexivity, or the ethnographer's use of inserting his or her experiences and feelings into the ethnographic process. This practice is not unique to postmodernism; it has been around in anthropology since the 1960s (in sociology at a later date), even earlier if one uses Malinowski's diary as a watershed mark (see discussion in chapter 2). Interpretive ethnography, practiced by Geertz (1973, 1983) and others, also made use of narrative and a certain reflexivity, but it used the method in an attempt to produce a cultural reality that was cultural member based (see the earlier section on interpretive ethnography).

Marcus (1999), perhaps the most outspoken postmodernist in anthropology, sees reflexivity as a concern not so much of method but of ideology—how one chooses to use reflexivity for intellectual and theoretical purposes. *Essential reflexivity* is a natural feature of human discourse, located in the everyday use of speech acts, framed in the broader context of language use. Postmodernism tries to harness this essential reflexivity and use it as a tool in creating a polyphonic text, one that speaks from the ethnographer to the cultural members and emphasizes all the voices, not just the dominant ones.

Because of this polyvoiced ethnography and, as Marcus labels it, "multi-sited nature of ethnography—where ethnography does not reside in the traditional 'one culture-one people' mentality," it is hard for the postmodern ethnographer to become anything but an outsider. Cultural members are never just inside or outside; they constantly skirt identity as they occupy different cultural sites. What is produced is then subjective, negotiated, in a fictional account that cannot reproduce the cultural reality of those being studied. To some, like George Marcus and James Clifford, ethnography is a humanistic literary device that is, at best, a text of the ethnographer's autobiographical journey through his or her experience. The unique personality of the ethnographer generates a highly individualized relationship between fieldworker and cultural members—one that provides insight but may only be realized through that particular fieldworker.

Interpretive Ethnography and Postmodernism: Reflexivity

If there is a difference between interpretivism and its radical offspring, postmodernism, it is the use of reflexivity—or the role of the ethnographer in fieldwork. Both acknowledge that the ethnographer plays a central role in the production of the fieldwork and ultimately the text. This is usually characterized through narrative (see the section on voice starting on p. 93), in which the ethnographer, through his or her experiences of fieldwork, sheds light on behavior of cultural members and his or her own behavior and helps trace some sense of cultural reality. But the interpretivism of Geertz and others, such as European sociologists Pierre Bourdieu and Anthony Giddens, uses the ethnographer's reflexivity to understand his or her behavior in terms of the ethnographer's cultural reality. The ethnographer can interpret symbols and meanings only by becoming deeply immersed in the culture. Eventually, the ethnographer can reach an understanding of symbol, meaning, and behavior of that culture and perhaps a better understanding of his or her reality as well. This hearkens back to our discussion of self and other (see chapter 3). The ethnographer studies other not in hopes of becoming other, but to understand other and then be able to communicate this other to members of the ethnographer's culture.

The postmodern use of reflexivity and narrative takes a different path. Postmodernists do not want to become totally immersed in a culture. In fact, they prefer to use their narrative as a means of a sitting on the fence that separates ethnographer from cultural member—refusing to enter into the fictional relationship of becoming, through extensive participation, a part of or even closely allied to other. At the same time, while maintaining a cultural distance, the ethnographer is more of a nomadic fieldworker, following a multisited strategy (Marcus 1999), building a composite view of cultural reality from the viewpoint of several identities that are reforming and reshaping as more traditional identities break down. This search for sites is contained within a confessional narrative of the ethnographer, creating a messiness of fieldwork. With no semblance whatsoever of a systematic analysis of the meaning of cultural reality, meaning and knowledge are arrived at in the playing out of the relationship between ethnographer and fieldworker. The narrative of the ethnographer, told in a story form with an emphasis on the "I" of the ethnographer, yields cultural representation and the means by which the ethnographer knows it. In the end, there is only the story, the narrative, and the experience of the fieldworker to provide the reader with knowledge of the culture and a view that has little explanatory power.

(Humanistic) Positivism

A *realist,* or *positivistic,* ethnography minimizes the amount of material that directly relates to the ethnographer's role in the text. The narrative takes on a third-person voice that usually plays down the emotion and passion of fieldwork. The goal of a positivistic ethnography is to describe and re-create a representation of cultural reality that is close to what that culture perceives. This typically includes a statement concerning the reason for undertaking fieldwork and a discussion of the theory of the behavior displayed and presented by cultural members. In effect, the ethnography advances discovery and explanation of cultural practices and behavior. Durrenburger (1999) labels this a "cultural" science—findings that others can use to advance knowledge of that human behavior.

Ethnography is a tool for a humanistic science. Durrenburger (1999) feels that ethnography helps people understand others as well as themselves. This process is a science of sorts, one driven by a culture's desire to understand the world around them. The scientific revolution that began in the 17th century was initially jump-started not by a theory, but by a new way of looking at the same old world. In effect, science is a cultural artifact; the method for discovery may change from culture to culture, but the application of the method that strives for understanding does not change. That is why, even in a field such as anthropology, ethnography can provide the means to formulate and analyze field data so that discovery, understanding, and a representation of cultural reality can be derived.

With the radical change and shifting of cultural boundaries and identities in today's world, ethnography offers a way to make these changes understandable. What was once an empirical world with closed boundaries, set identities, and few rigidly defined cultural realities is now (to postmodernists) a world featuring too many cultural realities with no outside universal reality. In studying sport and athletes across traditional boundaries, examples of "global" athletes emerge, or perhaps better yet, athletes claiming identities to sport companies. The athlete now has allegiance to many individuals and groups—parents and agents, teams and athletic sporting companies, nations and cultural communities. For positivists, cross-cultural universals in human behavior can be acknowledged using ethnography to attempt to compare cultures, even though the cultural landscape has been reconfigured and new cultural groups (such as athletes) have formed and are forming. The name of the game has changed, but the players, rules, and outcomes have not.

Although, or possibly because, the revolution of interpretivism and postmodernism has permeated academic fields, one thing is certain. Newly emerging disciplines such as literary criticism, feminist studies, cultural studies, and ethnic studies owe their academic voice to a postcolonial world. It can even be said that postmodernism has finally come home to roost in sport social sciences. A special issue of *Sociology of Sport Journal,* one of the two organs of the field (first issue, 2000), edited by Jim Denison and Robert Rhinehart (two self-acknowledged Norman Denzin disciples), presents the use of sociological narratives. In their introduction to the issue, they described their graduate days as kinesiology students sitting in Denzin's seminar at the University of Illinois as an experience that would make them committed to "making fictional and other types of storied representations an accepted form of scholarship" (Denison and Rhinehart 2000, 2).

That issue of *Sociology of Sport Journal* included examples of elements of postmodernism (also referred to as experimental ethnography), such as narrative and autoethnography (discussed later) and ethnographic fiction and poetry, once considered experimental methodology in anthropology that are now finding respectability in the arena of sport studies. Denison and Rhinehart present an array of narrative and fiction—female reporters in male locker rooms, high-performance sport, corruption in collegiate athletics, football fanaticism—to reveal "the power that evocative texts hold in representing the experience of others" (2000, 2). Echoing Denzin, the editors describe an in-depth and "complicated conceptual shift in the way one approaches subjects and topics," and echoing Clifford, "striving to be a work of literary achievement, artistically shaped and satisfying" (2000, 3).

It is interesting to note that I too spent three years in the kinesiology department at the University of Illinois before transferring back into anthropology to finish my PhD. While they were undergoing their semester-long epiphany in postmodernism in 1991, I was just across the quadrangle from Denzin's classroom turning my participant-observation narrative (combining voices of ethnographer and cultural members) of my sprint research into a dissertation that was a cognitive look at how sprinters ascribe identity.

Where Marcus and others see the social sciences adrift without the tie to a traditional theoretical orientation, searching for a paradigm to call their own, ethnography continues to produce the same kind of qualitative looks at cultural reality that it always has, in whatever designation constitutes a culture (see chapter 4). Each ethnography advances new or continued representations of these cultural realities. Durrenburger (1999) notes that what separates ethnography from other enterprises is that the text is valid. A view can be tested or at least reproduced and authenticated. A fieldworker has compiled actual experiences; they are not derived from secondary sources or made up.

Any ethnographer can be second-guessed, especially now when it is imperative the ethnographer alert the reader to cultural baggage he or she is lugging into the field. Bohannon and van der Elst see emotional dimensions in ethnography clouding the issues if not aired to the reader. Therefore, the fieldworker should admit his or her outside status while also reporting the inside view and emotions that surround that view. Any view lacking the emotions of the fieldworker will place the work in jeopardy of acceptance by academics and the cultural members (1999, 63).

Most important, an ethnographer's fieldwork and text represent, among other things, a record that can be examined. Other ethnographers produce their own records. This repeatability, a hallmark of any kind of scientific endeavor, allows for snapshots of cultural reality taken at different times by different cultural photographers to represent a composite reality. Obviously, different people and different angles of fieldwork will produce differing views of this reality. But these differing views will have more in common than not.

The work of Wheaton, Klein, and Bolin is valuable not so much for the information and cultural reality they advance or the view they construct, but because the work is authentic, derived only from the cultural members. Herein lies the primacy of ethnography: to understand those who are different but also similar. The experiences of the ethnographer and creation of the ethnography become the bridge between the two. Understanding those who are different is essential; the search for cultural meaning a necessary part of that understanding. The disparate views detailed in this chapter would seem to be synonymous. Richardson (2000) agrees that a storied account must contribute an understanding of social life. It would be hard to find an ethnographer who does not agree that in some ways, ethnography contributes to an understanding of a group of people. To Richardson (a postmodernist) the ethnography must also rest on its aesthetic value, the ethnographer's awareness of postmodern doctrine, the correct usage of reflexivity, and the emotional or intellectual effect of the work on the reader. The degree to which the ethnographer was viscerally subjected to a lived experience and moved to action become, along with style and look, the criteria by which to judge the merits of a piece of ethnography. It is not too difficult to see the influence of literary or creative arts in postmodern thought. Much emphasis is placed on how the ethnography was accomplished and how is it presented. I cannot help but wonder about the importance of the ethnographer in the production because it seems to supersede what ethnography has always been about, explanation. To this end, Richardson seems to present a premise that dovetails with positivism—does the text "embody a fleshed-out sense of lived experience? Does it seem true—a credible account of a cultural, social, individual and communal sense of the 'real'?" (2000, 16).

It may not be the ethnographer's role as a major player in the ethnography or even the appearance of the ethnography that makes it a useful tool in the process of explanation. The questions that emanate from the text that seek answers from other work portend the usefulness of ethnography. First, what makes a windsurfer culture? What are the premises or axioms that lay the foundation of windsurfers' shared cultural reality? Wheaton attempted to construct a cultural reality from her fieldwork. But why stop there? It is human nature to view the dissimilar and compare it to the similar or familiar.

Belinda Wheaton windsurfs in Hawaii: comparative fieldwork.

Are windsurfers in Great Britain similar to those of San Pedro, California (windsurfing capital of Southern California)? Do they have the same values and beliefs? Are there beliefs or values that are common to windsurfers everywhere? Wheaton's research describes a gender-driven culture, male dominated. Can the experiences that produced this conclusion be found elsewhere? Can one talk about a global windsurfing culture? Again, why stop there?

What are the similarities and differences between surfers and windsurfers? They share the same waters and dedication to pursuing their sport. Again, surfers as a culture have to be defined as such, extracting the commonalities that bind them together or noting the differences that create variations within. At each step of comparison, the cultures are uncovered as being defined by cultural boundaries and cross-cultural similarities. In a positivistic enterprise, understanding need not come from empiricism. Through validity and authenticity, any type of ethnography can accomplish a systematic analysis.

Writing Culture: Voice

In traditional ethnography, voice was consistently distanced and sterile of emotion and experience. Today, voice has become a legitimate concern for ethnography—how is culture reality presented and from what perspective is it described and made understandable? Narrative or third person, detached or collaborator, the voice (or presentation) of the ethnography becomes a defining feature. Distancing the ethnographer and the reader from the familiar by using a detached third person takes the subject outside the realm of the everyday cultural meanings. In this fictionalized space, the ethnographer and reader can survey the cultural landscape somewhat free of the entanglements of cultural baggage carried by both. H.G. Bissinger uses this kind of voice in *Friday Night Lights,* which describes the culture of Texas high school football. Instead of using an editorial voice, Bissinger attempts to present a picture not clouded by his judgment or overt morality. The stark portrayal of football and its impact on Odessa and Texas life did just that for the reader. John Feinstein's many books on highly visible sports and teams attempt the same presentational method, almost as if shot from a camera.

I have used the example of Hunter Thompson's *Gonzo* style of journalism[2] as a contemporary voice in producing a lively mode of cultural research. Alan Klein (1988) suggests that Thompson's work, due to its exaggeration of public views, makes sure to create distance between familiar and foreign. In many ways, Thompson's work can be thought of as a kind of ethnography. The venues he selects and his often raw and earthy prose acclimate the reader to an interpretation that borders on, or even creeps over into, the bizarre. In effect, he is writing on the fringe of culture. In past work (Sands 1999b, 1999c, and 1999d), I have described my ethnography as an attempt to incorporate Thompson's style, not so much for the bizarre but for the use of his person to act as a camera, always on, clicking stills or a video, letting the reader see the culture through the lens of his mind and ultimately his pen. Through participation in sprinting, football, or surfing, my aim was to let the reader feel the experience of participation as I did and at the same time begin to know the culture that the experience is encased in. This voice is different from classical research because it is not a distant or removed look. It is also different from interpretive or postmodern voices, which can lose interpretation in filters of translation. The voice produces a text that stands as one perspective, presenting a slice of experience alien to the readers. At the same time, for those who have experienced the participation and cultural experience before or are undergoing it at the time, the text produces a validation of experience or offers a new perspective on the familiar. In either case, the ethnography produces further knowledge on the workings of culture and the behavior of its participants.

The voice of the interpretist differs markedly from the classical voice through its use of a focused perspective. In its delivery, the voice of the interpretist makes the ethnographer more attentive to the exercised role of cultural mediator. This voice has moved ethnography away from the voice of authority and truth to one whose power lies in the art of fieldwork and as a literary text. The reader can interpret for himself or herself the reflexivity of the ethnographer. Rather than producing a truth, it produces an effort that lies between fiction and lived experience. Differing voices are similar in producing cultural translations of reality, but they differ in what can be done with the text.

Recently, a narrative style referred to as *autoethnography* has been introduced as "highly personalized, revealing texts in which the authors tell stories about their own lived experiences, relating the personal to the cultural" (Richardson 2000, 11). These lived experiences strain to be evocative and powerful in relating the author's (ethnographer's) experience to the reader. In a recent *Sociology of Sport Journal* issue, Andrew Sparkes (2000) recounts the difficulties of getting his autoethnographic account of struggling with a sport-related injury through the publication process. Sparkes writes about the prejudices of conservative and inflexible reviewers unable to see the scholarly merits of autoethnography as a legitimate research process. His article is primarily a treatment of the worth of autoethnography to contemporary ethnography and his attempts to write possible criteria for evaluating the merits of an autoethnography. One can also look at this research method as a life history living in the ethnographer's body. How different is the story from life history to autoethnography? If both were written in the first person or third person, can the reader distinguish between the two? Evaluating the merits of a particular work has always been a way to measure its worth. The criteria suggested by postmodernists such as Denzin, Marcus, Richardson, and others (as well as Sparkes) are based on features that speak to an egocentrism of the ethnographer, which has been the basis for their opposition to traditional ethnography. One is a call against omnipotence; the second position seeks to reject the power that lived experience holds over explanation. The revolution continues, and the battle lines remain the same.

Giulianotti's work on football hooliganism somehow mediates between single authority and community or polyphonic voice. There is the possibility of interpretation of the cultural members' narrative because the self who is narrating has been shaped and edited by cultural members. Thus, even the fieldworker who has spent considerable time in the field can argue that the narrative produced has undergone some of the same kinds of cultural shaping mechanisms. Hughson (1998) suggests ultimately that voice and ethnographic writing is about, as Hammersley and Atkinson argued, "strictly a balance" between the "concrete and the analytical" (Hammersley and Atkinson in Hughson 1998, 53).

Concluding Remarks

It is now clearer than ever that ethnography produces a unique form of qualitative data and analysis in social sciences. This chapter has been in part a simplistic explanation of the differing perspectives on how ethnography (its data, analysis, reflexivity, and voice) fits into contemporary social and cultural theory. The controversy that has emanated from the application of postmodern interpretation to ethnographic theory is one of bitter divide. It is clear, as suggested earlier, that the nature and limitations of ethnographic data preclude the use of an empirical scientific methodology. But a dominant thought remains that some kind of positivism is not only possible but necessary in the continued search to understand those who are different, or today, perhaps, only a little different. For this understanding to occur, it is suggested that ethnographers use some kind of reflexivity or fieldworker subjectivity. Producing cultural reality and understanding, however, does not have to be bathed in the harsh light of social criticism. Nor does ethnography need to become a statement of social activism. It is slightly ironic that the words written by Malinowski almost 100 years ago—"seeing life through the eyes of the native"—still describe a major goal of fieldwork and eventual text for many ethnographers.

I will suggest (in chapter 9), using my research on athletes, that it is indeed possible to combine the features of "realist" (van Maanen 1988) or positivistic ethnography and the reflexivity found in interpretive and postmodern ethnography. I label this method of "humanistic positivism" as *experiential ethnography* (mentioned earlier). The kinds of data found in sport—usually hidden to a nonparticipant—such as emotions, sensuous feelings and desires, and mental and physical pain, to name a few, can not only be retrieved from cultural members and the ethnographer but also stand in as acceptable kinds of data for a humanistic positivism.

One can say that the underlying role of ethnography, to paint a view of the culture, is satisfied by any kind of presentation or perspective. Acceptance and understanding of the ethnography and the view it presents hinges on the reader's perspective, experience, and cultural membership. It may be the reader's level of experience that affects how much information and perspective he or she gleans from the ethnography. Although the

ethnographer often approaches the ethnography as new and novel experiences—
and often perceives it that way—readers do not base their comprehension and
understanding of the material on the same principle. In the end, it may be that
ethnographic style, presentation, and interest dictate what the reader takes away
from the public view of culture.

Endnotes

1. For more information on this style of postmodern or interpretist voice,
   see Marcus and Fisher, *Anthropology as Cultural Critique* (Chicago:
   University of Chicago Press, 1996), Marcus, *Through Thick and Thin*
   (Princeton, New Jersey: Princeton University Press, 1999), Denzin
   and Lincoln, *The Landscape of Qualitative Research* (Thousand Oaks,
   California: Sage, 1998), and Denzin, *Interpretive Ethnography: Ethnographic Practices for the 21st Century* (Thousand Oaks, California: Sage, 1997).

2. See Thompson's classic work *Fear and Loathing on the 1972 Campaign Trail* and his brutal look at Las Vegas and the American dream,
   Fear and Loathing in Las Vegas, as examples of this style of voice.

Chapter 7

Risk and Ethnography

I am terribly overstrained, my work here seems all to be going to bits. There seems nothing here but Death—a man was dead in the village this morning of dysentery . . . In one village of 20, 9 died in one week . . . Spanish influenza has wiped out whole villages in Santo, Pentecost & Malekula, one might say districts. As for work, I dispair & dispair again.

—Bernard Deacon, ethnographer, in M. Gardiner's
Footprints on Malekula:
A Memoir of Bernard Deacon

Doing ethnography poses more risk than any other data-gathering methodology in the social sciences. The risk takes the form of the possibility of physical and emotional injury; exposure to a foreign disease; civil unrest and the danger of everyday life in places of marginality in society (crack neighborhoods in New York City); and so on. Part of doing good ethnography (completing fieldwork) is deciding what level of risk to bear. In sport ethnography, if participation is part of the fieldwork, physical injury is always a possibility. In my football research, my family was aware of the dangers of the sport and frequently reminded me of the risks in subtle and not-so-subtle ways. Exposure to such risks, however, makes the experience of participation more real to the ethnographer. The experience becomes a part of the cultural reality that is being formed through fieldwork.

This chapter will explore three areas of concern:

- Acknowledging the risk associated with ethnography
- Deciding what risk is acceptable
- Experiencing what you are studying

The Parable of Risk: A Rite of Passage

When dealing with the issue of risk in ethnography, I am reminded of two stories—one the plight of Wile E. Coyote in the Roadrunner cartoon, the other told to me by my track coach during my research on sprinters. While waiting for traffic to clear on a busy highway so that he could get to the infamous feathered speedster, the coyote took all the proper precautions, including looking both ways. The traffic thinned out and vanished. The coyote, now free of concern about danger from speeding cars and trucks, stepped out onto the tarmac and was crushed by an anvil dropped from the cliff above. The moral of the fable, that danger can lurk just around the corner, is apt for me on an eight-foot wave, or for Malinowski on the wings of malarial mosquito—even with safety observed to the utmost. I heard the second story from the sprint coach. Before an extremely hard practice, he told us the story of the sprinter who thought he could run himself to death. He ran and ran and ran and finally passed out. Then he woke up. The moral of the story is that no matter how hard or painful research can be, fieldwork ends.

Confronting and then successfully handling the risks implicit in fieldwork can also be thought of as a rite of passage.[1] All societies feature this notion of rites of passage—life stages that signal the passage of an individual into another position in the culture. A universal feature of these rites, especially for males, is the concept of enduring and overcoming pain and risk. For much of traditional ethnography, this risk took the form of traveling to distant and foreign lands and was symbolically cast as the image of the anthropologist being slowly lowered into a large pot over a fire tended by headhunters.

Whether the fieldwork includes complete participation or active observation, the ethnographer will at some point be placed—or choose to place himself or herself—in a situation that carries risk. Physical risk, even death, carries the "heroic" badge of courage and bravery. Still today, even after the colonial period, the value of the "'anthropologist as hero' has muffled, to a large degree, both the physical and psychological risks of fieldwork" (Miller 1999, 49). In anthropology, ethnographers never truly attained a sense of professional status in the eyes of their colleagues until they successfully completed their first fieldwork and all that it entailed. Malinowski may have been the first modern ethnographer to face risk. Malinowski accompanied the Trobrianders on fishing and interisland *kula* (ritual trading) expeditions in their seafaring canoes. Classical ethnographers certainly faced up to the dangers of fieldwork. Death, although not common, was a distinct possibility—if not from exotic diseases or foreign lifestyle, then from the risks associated with travel to and from these far-flung cultures. Many an ethnographer contracted contagious diseases, such as typhoid and malaria, that remained a living reminder of their fieldwork until their death.

Greater Risks

Some risks pose the danger of serious injury or death. These risks are somewhat removed from those that most sport ethnographers will face. Contemporary ethnographers still face the specter of instantaneous or contracted death. Michele Zimbalist Rosaldo lost her life when she slipped and fell off a slick path in the Philippines Highlands in the early 1980s. In the same period, British anthropologist Bernard Deacon, doing fieldwork on a South Pacific island, died of black water fever at the age of 24 a few days before his scheduled return from the island. Ironically, Deacon had been writing letters home to his fiancée about the prevalence of disease among those he was studying. Sadly, as this book goes to press, the continent that probably produced the most research on indigenous peoples, Africa, now poses the greatest risk to fieldworkers in the form of AIDS—one out of four people who live in Africa is HIV-positive.

One cannot ignore the reality that leaving a comfortable and somewhat predictable lifestyle will increase the risk of misfortune. But the ease of present-day world travel reduces both the danger found in classical ethnography and the mystique of fieldwork as a rite of passage and risk-laden adventure.

As for any world traveler, the risk of danger or even imminent death lurks in the volatility of social, ethnic, and civil violence in many world regions. South Africa has the highest crime rate of any Western country, Eastern Europe has been devastated by civil and ethnic unrest, and the guts of Africa have been reeling from civil and ethnic violence for years. Ethnographers could once claim some immunity in these areas because of their unique position, but no longer. In conflicts in which women and children guilty only by association are killed indiscriminately, ethnographers find themselves possible victims of the same fate.

Risks of the Familiar

With the emergence of new frontiers of cultural research, borders that were once drawn by political boundaries have now been supplemented, even replaced, by borders that invade the cultural life of the ethnographer. Risk can be found next door as well as down the block and over an ocean. John Sugdon, white and English, in his fieldwork on the boxing culture, spent time deep in Harlem and Ulster for his ethnography. His fieldwork was fraught with a constant acknowledgment of risk: "My spine would tingle each time I entered the field and my pulse would not return to its normal pattern until I had a few miles between myself and the boxing club's doors. . . . It was vitally important to keep this in mind and be aware of the dangers at all times, otherwise the doom filled predictions of my colleagues may well have come true" (1997, 230). In other studies, Sugdon, whom other ethnographers may feel has a death wish, relates experiences of chasing suspected car thieves and shady boxing promoters in a wild car chase, having a revolver pointed at his head by IRA terrorists in Northern Belfast, and witnessing a drug transaction while having a conversation at a bar in Havana. Admitting to everyday risks that we all must encounter and evade, Sugdon makes the point that ethnographers are out of their predictable daily patterns and in situations of heightened vulnerability because they are operating in political and social contexts where their cultural mastery is limited. "When we make the decision to undertake ethnographic research we are electing to step outside of these familiar and relatively secure routines and once we take to the field the chances of encountering threatening situations are increased" (Sugdon 1997, 241).

In their respective studies on football hooliganism, Giulianotti and Armstrong encountered physical risks. In studies of deviancy (such as their research), there is risk in gaining safe access to all in the culture. In this context, conflict between group members is always present. Such clashes may be especially perilous to one who enters with an agenda that might be construed as dangerous to or at odds with the culture and cultural members. Giulianotti's and Armstrong's fieldwork also included the possibility of arrest during situations where they encountered violence. An arrest would have affected their professional lives, of course, and time spent in jail or when being held for questioning would have affected their rapport with cultural members. Questions of loyalty and "narcing" to the authorities would have been real concerns of cultural members

Psychological risks can be just as haunting and just as long term as risks involving physical or bodily harm. Anthropologist Philippe Bourgois did fieldwork on the crack culture in East Harlem and resided in a seedy, drug-infested neighborhood for five years. Danger came from both the inside and the outside—he was mugged for eight dollars and verbally abused daily by the addicts who populated his days, and he was handled roughly by police who did not believe he was a professor doing research (Bourgois 1995). He experienced a shooting from his window, a bombing, a machine-gun shootout from an eatery, the tail end of a crack-house fire bombing, at least a dozen assaults, and "almost daily exposure to broken-down human beings, some of them in fits of crack-induced paranoia, some suffering from delirium tremens and others in unidentifiable pathological fits of screaming and shouting insults to all around them" (Bourgois 1995, 32). The risks of fieldwork were equaled by the danger of just surviving in such a location. In one way, his total emergence into that culture, his survival for the lengthy period of fieldwork, and his facing of those inherent dangers created an atmosphere that his subjects faced, giving him a richly textured, gritty, and realist view of street life for the drug addict. Daily risks ran high for both the addicts and the ethnographer.

Risk of Participation

For those involved in sport research, danger and risk apply not only to experiential participants but also to those who observe the competitions, games, tournaments, and matches. The thought that those not involved in complete participation (see chapter 9, "Experiential Ethnography") undergo little risk in studying sport does not take into account the changing nature of sport, as the world around sport changes as well. The image of an ethnographer sitting on rickety wooden bleachers watching teams battle on rutted, patchwork turf is just one fieldwork scenario. Gary Fine's ethnography of Little League baseball, *With the Boys: Little League Baseball and Preadolescent Culture,* fits this image. How risky is it to spend a summer watching 12-year-olds play America's pastime? Compared with 31 years ago, when I played, it is plenty risky. Today, parents abuse the officials and abuse the coaches. Many abuse the kids, and some assault each other. In one incident in 2000, a hockey father was killed by another hockey parent in Massachusetts. Youth football and soccer are no different. Would Fine today consider doing a project like the one he completed 15 years ago? Sport in America, at all levels, has become infused with a violence seen in the surrounding society. Figure skaters are beaten. Hockey players are charged with assault, even murder. As the profit and fame escalate, the stakes multiply, and the circumstances affect more than just the athletes.

Much work has been done in the last two decades on soccer hooliganism—any kind of participant-observation work would have included the ethnographer sitting in the middle of the fray. Soccer violence occurs in both Europe and Latin America. Spectators, including budding ethnographers, are at risk of fan violence, not to mention the unsafe physical state of stadiums and arenas.

The accelerating pace of global change has brought nations, ethnicities, and cultures into political and social conflict. Watching a cricket match in Johannesburg, South Africa, may not place the ethnographer in peril, but spending an extended time in South Africa to study the role of sport in South African ethnic relations will place the fieldworker in a society where the incidence of murder, rape, and violent crime is the highest in the world. Although not an ethnography, Rick Telander's classic book *Heaven Is a Playground,* about his summer of experiencing basketball in New York City, chronicles the culture shock he underwent. As stated above, the ethnographer is a foreigner, possibly not in citizenship but certainly in cultural belonging. Observing the culture of Julliard Music Academy would not present much risk, but placing your life in the hands of a New York cabbie to get to a Julliard concert might.

Risk in ethnography takes on psychological consequences, as experienced by Bourgois in New York City. "The practice of participant-observation [makes] . . . one factor clear, any ethnographer in learning new ways of looking at the world, risks immense emotional distress" (Bohannan and van der Elst 1999). Mari Womack spent a season in the dugout of the Los Angeles Dodgers doing fieldwork on professional sport. Her entrance to the field was her role as a journalist, but she underwent much torment as a female and a journalist doing her fieldwork (personal communication, March 1999).

At one time rare, political, social, and ideological violence have become almost an expectation at sporting events. Violence at international events has a long history, starting with the 1968 Mexico City Summer Olympics and continuing to the present day. As sport becomes a more common vehicle for international relations, the high visibility of participation by players and nationalities opens up the dangers that have become commonplace in other arenas of society.

The ethnographer can certainly minimize risks by observing the cultural etiquette of those being studied and taking pains to promote the trust and respect of the cultural members. The covert researcher probably assumes the greatest risk. Still, risk can be found simply in being in the wrong place at the wrong time. On the eve of my 64-year-old mother's departure to visit my brother who was working in Johannesburg, all six children questioned whether it was advisable for her to go. She responded that she was aware of the danger (in fact one of the first things my brother did was take her through Soweto) but that it would be more debilitating to her if she did not go. "If we are to let the risks of living in today's world dictate our travel and our experiences, then we have bowed to the fears that live within us. We have to slay those dragons ourselves," she told me after I expressed my fears of her going. Although most ethnographers do not look for dragons to slay, doing ethnography does entail facing the fear of the unknown. In a post-script, it is ironic that my mother was the one who expressed the most reservations about my playing college football at age 37. Go figure.

In a one-of-a kind systematic study, anthropologist Nancy Howell researched the health hazards and risk involved in fieldwork. In her 1990 book *Surviving Fieldwork,* Howell thought of her project as illuminating the costs of doing ethnography. With moral and financial backing from the American Anthropological Association (AAA), she sampled 331 anthropologists and found, among other things, that males and females have equal hazard frequency and that Africa had the highest hazard frequency. Her work also produced a look at rarely expressed topics such as mental health.

Playing the Game: Well Worth the Risk

Good investigative or undercover journalists, if asked how far would they go in getting the story, would no doubt answer, "As far as it takes." In some ways, ethnographers are no different. They must gauge fieldwork and decide either to accept the risks posed or to deflect or minimize the risks through an altered strategy. But the ethnographer is after a two-year story, and deflecting or minimizing risk can produce a story different in scope and breadth. In participant (experiential) sport ethnography, the risks are the same as those encountered by the athletes themselves.

In my track research, I suffered a pulled hamstring my first season and spent six weeks recuperating and going through physical therapy. Looking back, if an injury can be fortuitous, that hamstring pull was. For six weeks, I was able to experience the worst possible scenario to a sprinter, pulling a muscle and being unable to compete. I was able to observe and experience the dark side of competition and produce a slice of sprinting reality not usually probed in depth. This is not to say that injury or risk needs to be actualized, but the ethnographer must accept the risk. In many ways, this ethnographer's risk management is accepted and then internalized by other cultural members, aiding the establishment of rapport (see discussion on rapport in chapter 3).

Accepting the risk of injury, even possible death, in the participant sporting method is somewhat different than assuming the risks of doing fieldwork in New York City drug neighborhoods or sailing over open ocean in a *kula* canoe. For one, the risks of sport, even the less physically demanding sports—in bowling lurk back pains and overworked wrists—are continual and wrapped up in the fabric of the activity. Because participation requires the constant vigil of seeking the experience of sport, the participant accepts

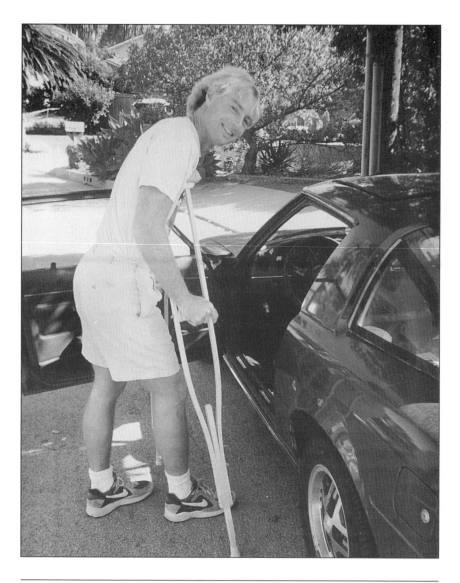

Risks are commonplace for players and ethnographers. Here I am recovering from a severely pulled groin muscle during my first football season, 1994.

the physical risk after a while, with little fear of danger. Second, risk, injury, and the tolerance of pain actually define the participant as an active member of that population of athletes, characterized by words that hang above every locker-room door, "No pain, no gain." As any sport experiential ethnographer will tell you, injury and pain is not a question of if, but when. By stepping onto the field, playground, or surfline, you may feel a flutter or gust of fear that signals risk, but to you as an ethnographer, the risk of injury may be far less than the risk of not following through with your study. Can there be anything worse in academics, or to your soul, as failing?

Concluding Remarks

In today's litigation-happy world, there is no such thing as a waiver absolving responsibility or accepting responsibility of risk encountered while in the field. No insurance is available for fieldwork. I conclude this chapter typing with knuckles that remain swollen four years after I caught my last pass. I have a shoulder that still hurts when I try to lift my arm over my head. On good days, I look at them as my badges of courage, endured in the rites of passage I would never have experienced had I sat in the stands. On bad days, when I know I have only speeded up the onset of arthritis, I see these reminders as products of a misguided mind and a foolish heart. But even then, I comfort myself knowing that I share these injuries with former teammates. To this day, I experience the cultural reality of college football.

What was once the image of the intrepid ethnographer, alone in a foreign land and facing the risk of unfamiliarity as well as danger, can now be applied to the countless people who traverse the globe looking for vacation spots. Today, for most of us, living in a volatile and violent world, risk is as close as a freeway a mile from home, the nearest ATM, the neighborhood convenience store. For the ethnographer danger and risk lurk within the familiar and near as well as in a far-flung island culture. Doing good ethnography means accepting risks and knowing that exposure to risks sweetens the field experience and provides greater understanding of cultural behavior. Doing good ethnography also means being smart when deciding what risks are beyond good judgment. To quote the ad slogan of the 1990s, "Know when to say when."

Endnotes

1. In chapter 9 I will suggest that in an experiential ethnography, the ethnographer travels through a number of doors, each like a rite of passage, in search of cultural meaning. See also J. Peoples and G. Baily, *Humanity* (Belmont, California: Wadsworth, 2000, p. 73).

Chapter 8

Ethical Ethnography

The researcher has a moral obligation to consider possible re-percussions of the investigation and to communicate them to informants, making sure they understand.

—Daniel Bates and Elliot Fratkin, *Cultural Anthropology*

The colorful past of ethnography includes the demise of colonialism and the use of ethnographers to help identify and describe indigenous culture to colonial administrators. The past also entails the enlistment of ethnographers by the United States government to help understand the German and Japanese cultures during World War II and subvert communism during the Cold War and Vietnam Conflict. These periods opened the eyes of cultural researchers matriculating during the 1960s and 1970s to the responsibility of protecting their informants and people being studied as a first priority, even over politics and perceived patriotism.

In 2000 Patrick Tierney published *Darkness in El Dorado,* a scathing critique of two powerful scientists, anthropologist Napoleon Chagnon and geneticist James Neel, and their three decades of work with the Yanomamo of the South American rainforest. Chagnon's research on the Yanomamo is classic, as are his ethnographies that describe them as the Fierce People, a group for whom warfare and raiding are seemingly endemic. At some point in any undergraduate anthropology program, a student will read a book by Chagnon about his research and exploits in the Amazon jungle. Chagnon has described his intimate encounters with the Indians, living as a native for extended periods, using hallucinogens, and being given a Yanomamo name. Tierney's accusations—duplicity, staging of fieldwork situations, sexual impropriety by Chagnon and others doing fieldwork with the Yanomamo, orchestrating tension that led to violence for the sake of research—created a firestorm of controversy and painted anthropologists as highly unethical, selfish, opportunistic meddlers. Chagnon's arrogant and abrasive personality, which had not endeared him to his colleagues, did not help matters. Immediate response by the American Anthropological Association urged anthropologists to conduct fieldwork with standards of ethical behavior above reproach. Since the publication of *Darkness in El Dorado* in November 2000 and a special session devoted to Tierney and his book at the yearly convention of the American Anthropological Association, the allegations have been countered by support from numerous anthropologists. Many of Tierney's charges have been relegated to theory and conjecture. Whatever the outcome of this nasty debate, and it will rage for years to come, anthropological fieldwork has again come under scrutiny. This time it is not an internal audit but one that has been launched from outside the ivy walls. In a nutshell, fieldwork that once was thought to be a privilege and a right of anthropology has now come into alignment with the economical, political, and hegemonic reality of a 21st century world.

The issue of ethics in ethnography dovetails with the issues of theory (discussed in chapter 5) and produces just as much controversy. Once characterized by distinct boundaries, and often isolated by geography and cocooned in private space, cultures are today much more public and elastic in form. Changed as well is the relationship between ethnographer and cultural member. Once driven by a one-way interaction, in which information flowed from informant to ethnographer, the relationship is now more complex and often construed by both ethnographer and cultural member as a two-way interaction. To add to this milieu of change, the necessity and even the ethics of the overt nature of fieldwork have been questioned. Ethnographers tread into this uncertain 21st century realm—some lightly, others with the presence of a bull in a china shop.

This chapter will look at the following issues of ethics in ethnography:

- The relationship between ethnographer and cultural member
- Overt and covert ethnography
- Ethnographic intent and informed consent
- Public versus private knowledge
- The means by which cultural knowledge is elicited
- The use of cultural knowledge
- Sensitivity

Ethnographer and Cultural Member: A Dance of Natural Tension

Simply put, one of the main goals of the ethnographer is to elicit from an informant, or cultural member, information that the ethnographer either does not know or needs to have clarified. If doing this were as easy as asking directions to a restaurant from one who lives nearby, ethnography would be a snap—but it is not. The ethnographer intrudes on the cultural members' lives by constantly asking questions—many of them personal—and spending hours and hours watching, observing, and even participating in their lives. These behaviors affect the cultural members' lifestyles and often change their cultural behavior. The ethnographer then writes a book about them and makes money (what little money there is for academic texts), while the cultural members keep only memories of the fieldwork and the personality of the ethnographer.

Traditional ethnography followed on the coattails of colonialism. The ethnographer, in the guise of science, constructed a living laboratory out of the field site—watching and passively participating in the culture to pose, support, or falsify theories of human behavior. But as diligently as the ethnographer tried to achieve empirical objectivity, the nature of the relationship was fraught with the complexities and frailties that usually characterize relationships between friends. Attempting to pose fieldwork in such an objectivity created tension. The ethnographer tried to advance a body of work based on traditional scientific aims while becoming intensely immersed in a foreign culture, usually isolated from the familiar. It was difficult not to develop lasting friendships with the "natives," all the while trying to maintain the necessary self-versus-other relationship needed for an objective and distant perspective.

In other words, the one-way street does not exist in ethnography. In an open (overt) or covert method (see the next section for a discussion of the merits of both), the ethnographer must attempt to build a trusting and open relationship with cultural members. Whether the informant or cultural members realize or recognize the true intent of the ethnographer, soliciting accurate cultural information and immersing in cultural experience demands open and honest communication. It is almost impossible to spend two years in the field without establishing close friendships with some or many cultural members.

Postmodernists see positivistic ethnography as science cloaked in the notion of fieldwork serving the public good. Even though the shackles of colonialism have been thrown off, the ethnographer still represents the traditional capitalist order, taking the culture from the members for the benefit of the ethnographer and Western science. To combat this hegemony, postmodernists such as Norman Denzin see ethnography working for the good of the culture and people studied. In fact, to label it as "research" or a "study" is a misnomer. In an ethnography that Denzin defines as a "feminist, communitarian ethical model," the ethnographer is "personally involved, politically committed and not the morally neutral observer of positivism" (Denzin 1997, 274). Feminists historically have rejected positivism and scientific objectivity as a theory and method tied to white Western male anthropologists. Postcolonial theory and postmodern discourses have forced this *malecentric* bloc of anthropologists and other social scientists to reflect on their "otherness" and the centralist position of a malecentric authority. To many feminists, such as Wheaton (personal communication, June 27, 2000) and Bell (1993), this movement toward gender awareness is still in its infancy, and gender-blind ethnography continues to monopolize research and publication. According to Denzin, the fieldworker becomes social activist. Thus, because the ethnographer is committed to action that would benefit the members of the culture where fieldwork occurs, friendly, cooperative relations define such inquiry and the ethnographer becomes part of and serves the community studied.

In any case, the relationship between the ethnographer and cultural member is critical to the advancement of fieldwork. Cultural members hold the key to unlocking what goes on inside their minds and to decoding the behavior that they express in everyday life. The approach to discovering or uncovering the behavior that drives cultural reality is a critical component of the research strategy.

Research Strategies: Overt Versus Covert

From 1969 to 1971, anthropologist Dan Rose, then a graduate student at the University of Pennsylvania, "infiltrated" a black Philadelphia neighborhood, doing covert research while maintaining a job as an auto mechanic in a privately owned garage. His decision to seek field data in a clandestine manner was precipitated by the desire not to affect the natural flow of information and cultural knowledge that emanated from the cultural scenes of the neighborhood. He also decided that access to the "stuff" that made up the priceless field data was worth the effort it took to design and set up the "pragmatics of the field situation" (Rose 1987, 23). Well-known sociologist Irving Goffman was Rose's advisor. Goffman suggested that Rose "creatively manage" his identity within the field and locate a job within the neighborhood. To the unknowing participants, considering the period, Rose and his wife—who was accompanying him—would be hippies, dropping out of life for a while. To Rose, "what he [Goffman] was proposing was that we become undercover agents for scientific purposes" (Rose 1987, 21).

Against his principles, Rose adopted Goffman's suggestion and spends a chapter of his book revealing the anguish of the decision-making process.

Ultimately Rose chose to work covertly because of the challenge, "to collapse our identities insofar as possible into theirs, struck me directly . . . Although I could not then reconcile my feelings of conflict, anger and resentment, I told Goffman we [his wife as well] would do it" (1987, 21). Rose also saw the advantages to deep and complete immersion and the lack of entanglements of living a dual personality of ethnographer and participant. Also, to Rose, traditional and overt ethnography is focused on the overriding interests of the ethnographer, and these interests act to break up and disturb the everyday flow of interaction and cultural activity.

In a covert situation, accessing knowledge happens in the maddeningly slow pace of everyday life. The covert ethnographer cannot expend too much energy or zeal to discover or uncover the machinations of cultural behavior or the shared image of cultural reality. In other words, the ethnographer must live within the hidden identity to gain knowledge. To step out of character at any time would destroy the covert role so painstakingly put in place. Asking questions, posing hypothetical situations, or directing interviews and life histories are out of bounds to the covert fieldworker. Knowledge comes when and where the fieldworker can obtain it within the position of one who is a part of the social network for ordinary reason.

Rose published his work a full 15 years after his research. In a retrospective he wrote unhesitatingly that he would not choose that methodology in the future. The pain of covert work created frustration and despair that only avoidance, not diligence, could mute. During his fieldwork, Rose was full of anxiety of being uncovered or "made," the possibility of which haunted his daily life. He feared that the kind of data he was accessing was insufficient and not the kind needed for ethnography. He was also forced (or he chose) to participate in a method that went against the principles that were integral to his perception of his identity as an anthropologist and ethnographer. Despite these personal difficulties, however, as he was writing his book he was left with the feeling that being covert detracted from his ability to gain information and knowledge in natural course of events. "I came to think that the event as a unit of analysis did violence to the lived reality of everyday life and distorted rather than revealed the temporal grounds of interaction and social life" (1987, 29).

Overt Strategy

Thirty years after Rose completed his fieldwork, the issue of whether the ethnographer should inform those being studied is still hotly debated. The spirit of morality and the ethical implications of deliberately misleading those who are providing cultural information for a study (whether or not they realize they are providing information) reach back to the golden age of ethnography when ethnographic work fed the colonial powers. In 1970—well before ethnography had become the method of choice for qualitative research by other social sciences and cultural studies fields—in an effort to correct this notion and police themselves, the American Anthropological Association (AAA) adopted a code of ethics concerning the responsibility of the ethnographer to protect the rights of those being studied. A corollary to this code of ethics was the premise of informed consent, requiring the ethnographer to inform the cultural members of the research project and the potential ramifications of the study after its completion and then ask their consent to be featured as part of the study. This principle has since become the standard by which cultural research has been held accountable in anthropology and is required for research being done through universities or granting agencies. Informed consent has also since become an integral part of the codes of ethic of both the American Sociological Association (ASA) and the British Sociological Association (BSA) (see sidebar for the AAA and ASA code dealing with informed consent).

Informed Consent From the American Anthropological Association Code of Ethics

Anthropological researchers should obtain in advance the informed consent of persons being studied, providing information, owning or controlling access to material being studied, or otherwise identified as having interests that might be impacted by the research. It is understood that the degree and breadth of informed consent required will depend on the nature of the project and may be affected by requirements of other codes, laws, and ethics of the country or community in which the research is pursued. Further, it is understood that the informed consent process is dynamic and continuous; the process should be initiated in the project design and continue through implementation by way of dialogue and negotiation with those studied. Researchers are responsible for identifying and complying with the various informed consent codes, laws, and regulations affecting their projects. Informed consent, for the purposes of this code, does not necessarily imply or require a particular written or signed form. It is the quality of the consent, not the format, that is relevant.

Approved June 1998.

Informed Consent From the American Sociological Association Code of Ethics

Informed consent is a basic ethical tenet of scientific research on human populations. Sociologists do not involve a human being as a subject in research without the informed consent of the subject or the subject's legally authorized representative, except as otherwise specified in this Code. . . . When informed consent is required, sociologists inform research participants or their legal representatives of the nature of the research; they indicate to participants that their participation or continued participation is voluntary; they inform participants of significant factors that may be expected to influence their willingness to participate (e.g., possible risks and benefits of their participation); and they explain other aspects of the research and respond to questions from prospective participants. Also, if relevant, sociologists explain that refusal to participate or withdrawal from participation in the research involves no penalty, and they explain any foreseeable consequences of declining or withdrawing.

Revised spring 1997.

Legal and bureaucratic barriers have complicated and made ethnography, at least in anthropology, much more difficult than it was for Malinowski and others doing classical ethnography at the turn of the century. If the goal was to inform the cultural members that they are soon to be a part of a study, then the spirit—not necessarily the letter—of the premise of informed consent would seem to be acceptable. The early statements of conduct (AAA) stressed the need for written permission or waivers, but recent revisions realize that written forms may not always be possible and as long as consent is appropriated to the satisfaction of both parties, the letter of the code has been achieved. "It is the quality of the consent, not the format, that is relevant" (AAA code).

Ethnographers coming of age in this legally oriented society fall into the problem of applying their own cultural standards to other cultures. By shying away from digging for cultural reality, by not asking questions because of embarrassment or concern about intruding, the fieldworker is giving in to the fear of legal issues down the road as an excuse for doing poor ethnography or worse yet, no ethnography. Common sense would indicate that if the fieldworker intrudes on the privacy or personal space of cultural members, they would let the ethnographer know, through cultural practices or behavior, that their toes are being stepped on.

In the ethnographic trenches, after the fieldworker has established some kind of trust with cultural members, it is surprising to find that the opposite is true. People love to talk about themselves, about others, about their beliefs. The problem is more about when and how to turn off the faucet of cultural information that continually flows. In reality, most will be appreciative of the chance to talk, or even grateful for the opportunity to lend their experience to the ethnographer's growing body of accumulated knowledge. In all my research, I informed cultural members of my position as a researcher and participant. During these studies, I have found that athletes love to talk, mostly about themselves, but also about their skills and their sport. In the end of my basketball research, the beer I bought as an inducement to get players to talk was being consumed more by me than the players. Sprinters would come to practice early to sit on the pole-vault Porta Pits and talk to me about themselves, and I would have no trouble asking any of them to sit down and talk on a moment's notice. But the football players broke the mold of gushing informants. Faced with at least 60 players, many more than I had in either of my earlier ethnographies, I was constantly listening to players unload their thoughts on me—on the field, in the huddle, in the locker room, at parties, in bars. It wasn't long before players would search me out to tell me a thought or follow up an earlier conversation. I rarely had to do the opposite. This openness and desire to pass on information was aided, not hindered, by the knowledge that I was a cultural researcher–ethnographer doing participant observation. The fact that they knew I was doing research provided an open channel of communication and gave me access to much more information than I would have been privy to had I been covert in my research.

Doing ethnography does not harm the cultural members. The use of some information gathered in the course of research might prove to be harmful, but only if the ethnographer is not ethical or is simply insensitive in deciding what would harm or not harm the group. Harm can also occur if the ethnographer has a political or personal agenda that overrides the first premise of ethnography—gathering knowledge for knowledge's sake. To protect the identity of informants, many ethnographers choose to use pseudonyms for the cultural members and blur the location of the group.

For his beginning chapters in *Little Big Men,* Alan Klein chose to create a fictional gym in his work on bodybuilders, mostly to enhance anonymity for his cultural members and ensure privacy for his informants. In outside

Overt fieldwork: as I continued my study of sprinters at Santa Barbara City College in 1994, to my teammates, I was a sprinting anthropologist.

interviews with nationally known figures in that culture, he altered personalities and names to mask identity. Klein believes that creating a single site (his study included four gyms) aided the reader by generalizing into placement just one gym setting.

I chose to identify cultural members in all my research. All voluntarily chose to participate and be part of the research. As a result, changing identity and being vague in location would have been counterproductive. They were real people, complete with emotions, thoughts, performances, and desires. Not acknowledging their identity, to me, slighted their efforts and the time they gave to the project. Today, ethnography is not just for academia; it is also for the people who ethnographers study. Covering up identity reduces or minimizes the venture and knowledge of the cultural members. Many athletes involved in my studies wanted to be part of the research and the text, both to legitimize that culture and to validate their identity as athlete and student.

Covert Fieldwork

The ethical cannons of anthropology and sociology have little leverage over ethnographers in other fields of academic enterprise. With the rise of fields such as feminist studies, ethnic studies, gay studies, cultural studies, and applied anthropology, and the influence of postmodernism, the ethnographer's politics and personal agenda can become a motivation and reason for fieldwork. The ethnography can become a treatise in support of a stance in a rapidly changing and fracturing world order.

Covert research then becomes a necessity for accessing information or data for the ethnography, and ultimately for establishing a social or political agenda. Ethnography departs from academic manifestos, position papers, and books on political and social ideology in the intense nature of fieldwork and the need to build a trusting, respectful relationship with the cultural members under study. In covert research, the ethnographer in effect obtains cultural knowledge through a process of misrepresentation and deception, maintains an underlying hidden agenda, and *consciously* intends to use the field data in a way potentially harmful to the culture. The question of whether cultural knowledge should be considered private and off-limits without consent of those who possess or have ready access to it may be pertinent here. In this age of instantaneous cyber knowledge, ownership of any kind of knowledge may soon be a matter of a click of a mouse. When that happens, covert research will become overt, and the only kind of private knowledge will be that which never leaves your lips (see further discussion on knowledge in the next section).

Instead of taking the unbending position of requiring informed consent for every research situation, many researchers feel that the integrity (and common sense) of the fieldworker and the specifics of the field situation—the personality of the ethnographer, the culture under study, the cultural scene where research occurs, the intended use of cultural information and knowledge—should dictate the type and openness of the research methodology. The ASA does include a caveat in their code that sidesteps the issue of consent.

Despite the paramount importance of consent, sociologists may seek waivers of this standard when (1) the research involves no more than minimal risk for research participants and (2) the research could not practicably be carried out were informed consent to be required (ASA Code of Ethics).

An example of covert research in sport studies is Belinda Wheaton's covert, and later overt, study of the windsurfing culture (subculture to her— see chapter 4 for a discussion of the concept of culture) in the United Kingdom. Her research method included a "complete participant role" (Wheaton 1997, 163); she was already a participating member of that culture. Wheaton used a research method similar to one I used and others have engaged in (see chapter 9 for a discussion of complete participation): "The researcher cannot pass as a group member, s/he must become one" (from Hammersley and Atkinson 1997 in Wheaton 1997, 164).

In her work, Wheaton used a mixture of strategies, both overt and covert, to obtain information. She acknowledges that some commentators on this issue disavow ethical considerations, going as far to argue that deception is essential to do good research in a world where being unethical seems to be the operating norm. On the other hand, the practice of informed consent, in the guise of a simple piece of paper, does not necessarily preclude practices by the ethnographer that are unethical. Hidden research was necessary for her to enter a small, intimate, male-dominated culture. Complete participation, in terms of commitment and ability, gave her a leg up in that culture, but explicitly making known her research would have severely compromised her efforts to gain access to the culture and to informants.

Perhaps more germane to the question of morality is the degree of openness an ethnographer expresses in his or her relationships with cultural members. Bohannon and van der Elst, critical of current academic paranoia, write of ethnographers and anthropologists who complain that "only journalists can do classical anthropological fieldwork with impunity" (1999, 57). In the end, Wheaton decided that telling half-truths, providing information about the research only if asked, rationalized the practice. In reality, in an informal setting like the beach with a nomadic group of windsurfers, obtaining informed consent was problematic. "In practice, my initial role was insider and 'covert,' if people asked me what I was doing I told them—but in the main, they weren't interested—and I didn't go about publicizing the fact" (Wheaton, personal communication). In fact, her covert status disappeared once she began the process of formal and informal interviewing.

Alan Tomlinson's work with oral histories reflects a tension between the dubiousness and questionable authenticity of an informant played out against the background of other collected histories. The decision of Tomlinson to provide a consistent history, no matter what the effect on the relationship of the researcher and informants, was an "act of cultural survival that is achieved by reporting real passions, authentically disputational cultures, and doing so by reporting the real names of real people for whom such cultures were so important" (Tomlinson 1997, 261).

In anthropology, a discipline born on the backs of foreign cultures and the decidedly nonfamiliar and with a long history of conscious or unconscious hegemony and colonialism, the issue of informed consent serves to remind us of our sometimes-conflicting roles as humans and ethnographers. Academic fields now learning about the power of ethnography in discovery and description are also beginning to understand the power of the same ethnography for rationalizing social and political agendas. In losing sight of its foundation of seeking knowledge for knowledge's sake, ethnography leaves the familiar table of academia and steps into a global morass of shifting and changing cultural reality.

Belinda Wheaton's decision to embark on covert research was one not reached lightly or without personal anguish. She faced the same issues described by Rose in his research. Indeed, fieldworkers in sport studies experience research limitations, such as gender, race, ethnicity, and possibly performance skills, that will affect and chart the course of data gathering. When research designs give cultural members only enough information to allow the research to go forward, half-truths may be necessary. To constrain and alter the relationship of fieldworker and cultural members and the natural flow of information, even before the fieldwork has started, by introducing a written consent form speaks volumes about our society. It reflects the cultural practices and trust shared by other cultures. In the era of writing ethnography for multiple audiences, especially the audience of those studied, consent is an implicit part of research. Changing names to protect the innocent or unknowing is a way of removing the onus of moral responsibility of the ethnographer.

To me, ethnography is not only an academic and professional endeavor but also a personal revelation of others and the fieldworker. As Rose and Wheaton experienced as complete participants, living fieldwork can be much different from traditional participant observation. For two years or more (in each of my studies), I worked openly to establish a trusting and respectful relationship with all cultural members. To do so under a covert umbrella was something that ran counter to the spirit of ethnography, or the need to bring the culture and subjects to life. Many cultural members become lifelong friends, some become lifelong enemies, but that is life. Ethnography is not for everybody, nor should it be. It involves a blend of patience, understanding, and trust—qualities that supposedly make good humans.

Unlike Rose or Wheaton, I chose my research fields knowing that a deceptive course of research was not necessary. In their shoes, I might have selected a covert research strategy after undergoing similar internal conflict. I enjoyed and profited from their research and writing about both the cultures and their research strategies.

Public Versus Private Knowledge

With concern over the rights of those being studied and the harm that can come to individuals, even cultures, from disseminating ethnographic information, the question of whether rights and restrictions should be accorded to cultural knowledge garners much discussion among cultural researchers. Fueling this discussion is the legacy of conscious or unconscious exploitation of cultural members by cultural researchers. For example, ethnographers make money from their ethnographies of the Native American condition and then leave, doing little to correct the glaring inequities that exist between their lives and those that surround them (Bohannan and van der Elst 1999).

With this reasoning a moral decision has been made—that culture is the property of the cultural members and that this property can then be owned and, in a capitalistic sense, sold to the highest bidder. Thus, with this thinking, knowledge—the essence of what is learned and what generates behavior—is a private commodity that becomes public only when an exchange is made. True, what separates cultures is distinctness. Knowledge and culture belong to those who can understand it and, more important, to those who take the time and effort to learn what makes up the distinctness.

Culture is free; no laws or rights control or legislate who can and cannot learn culture. John Bale and Joe Sang wrote a book detailing the most dominant group of male (and as well female) long-distance runners in the world, the Kenyan runners. The success of the Kenyans has been described from first-person accounts, by scientific theory, by cultural determinism, and from many interviews with the runners and national coaches. Genes, altitude, race, diet, a combination of those factors, and even the Kenyans' belief that running is in the tribal Kenyan soul have been suggested at one time or another to account for their mastery. Beyond the lay and purely scientific desire to understand the Kenyans' success is the quest by groups or individuals who are not dominant in running to discover what factors create that success, to decode and decipher the secret formula. Bob Kennedy, the premier American 5,000 and 10,000 runner, trains with the Kenyans. He has said that the secret of their success is that they literally run themselves to death, and then to victory.

The reason or reasons for their dominance certainly are founded in their culture, available for any interloper or interested party to untangle, from one like Kennedy wishing to tap into some of that brilliance to those interested in understanding the limits of human performance. Kenyans are not genetic machines, nor are they culturally manufactured at the risk or suppression of their humanity. Understanding the culture serves best as a means for opening the different, the unique, and the unknowable to others; ethnography provides a tool for understanding those differences. When culture becomes commodified, owned, or restricted, misunderstanding through ignorance leads to racism and xenophobia. The more we learn of each other, the more common ground we create for understanding.

Sensitivity

In the current political and social environment, fieldwork may, in all likelihood, involve invading or stepping on the toes of groups, organizations, and cultural, ethnic, or racial groups. Defining what is sensitive and what is not becomes a matter of where or with whom fieldwork is done and the belief and value system of cultural members. Sensitive issues and concerns in one culture may be less sensitive to another culture. The sensitivity of a topic may even apply to groupings of cultural members within the culture itself. In other words, deciding what is sensitive requires spending much time with cultural members and using a whole lot of common sense. In the AAA code of ethics, anthropologists are advised that the cultural beliefs of official agencies, such as governments, should be respected. In many cases, ethnographers are guests of the culture.

Because most work on sport and culture to this point has involved fieldwork within Western society or like-minded cultures, the ethnographer is privy to issues and topical areas that pose concerns of sensitivity. A few areas that are controversial in contemporary sport studies are feminism and racism. Public and academic consumption of topics such as racial determinism in sport performance has approached taboo status. On the other hand, this topic has exposed the nerve endings of a subject that has an old and bitter history dating back to African colonialism and slavery. Recent work in this area, such as NBC's Tom Brokaw-hosted *Black Athlete: Fact and Fiction,* John Hoberman's (1997) *Darwin's Athletes,* and most recently Jon Entine's (2000) *Taboo,* has stirred up research and theories that collide head-on in both popular and academic arenas. Both Hoberman and Entine brought their work to recent NASSS (North American Society for Sport Sociology) annual conferences, where the emotions and feelings of academics surfaced in a cacophony of recrimination and even disgust. Often lost in the swirl of emotions—especially when dealing with gut-wrenching subjects like race, specifically that introduced by Hoberman and Entine—is the rigorous, in-depth academic critique that books, journals, and conference papers have provided for several decades. Writers of these critiques have had the chance to sit back and marshal thoughts and research, away from the eye of the hurricane. In this instance, the idea of taboo, or thoughts and opinions too sensitive to research on the subject of race, genes, and performance, was only partially applicable. This discussion and exchange of ideas created a controversy similar to that caused by Arthur Jensen's work on racial IQ, a divisive issue for psychologists and sociologists. In research I have done on black collegiate sprinters and college football players, however, the issue of racial performance was a topic that many athletes wished to discuss, and sensitivity was not a factor. I found that the athletes, although less informed about research studies and contemporary theory, were open-minded and forgiving of the positions of others.

Many questions are raised, and should be raised, about the content of research as well as the reception of research and theories. Perhaps the real question is whether some topics are too sensitive to broach, not only in research but also in discourse between academics. Pat Griffin's (1998) *Strong Women, Deep Closets* and Mariah Nelson's (1994) *The Stronger Women Get, the More Men Love Football* are two works that methodically challenge malecentrism and expose a patriarchy that has a stranglehold on women's sports. Griffin's book, however, contains many formal and informal interviews with female athletes and coaches that analyze the discrimination and prejudice against lesbians in the sporting experience—prejudice not only from administrators and coaches, many of whom are males, but also from the athletes themselves. Similar to race and performance issues in sport in general, the issue of sexual orientation has become a divisive concern in female sport. Many would suggest that the issue is sensitive, or even out of bounds of such discourse.

In today's public society, a far greater emphasis is placed on exposing topics that would have been considered too sensitive 20 or 30 years ago. In many ways, this public forum has desensitized topics and accelerated, at times forced and shaped, the way academics consider such concerns. As Barbara Miller writes, "The sheer sensitivity of a topic does not always imply that it is beyond the scope of a sensitive researcher!" (1999, 49). Ethics aside, doing good ethnography must include the ethnographer's common sense of minimizing potential harm and the obligation to protect the cultural members and the lives that he or she invades for such a long period. It will always be left to the ethnographer and the final text to do the right thing.

Chapter 9

Experiential Ethnography

Kinetic ethnography is . . . an active, productive process, rather than a passive recording of others' behaviors and beliefs.

—Larry de Garis

E thnography has become more than a tool for many cultural researchers; it has often become a way of life or a statement about the ethnographer's personal beliefs. Postmodern ethnography, labeled experimental or alternate ethnography when first introduced by Marcus and Fisher (1996), offers a number of research methods that 30 years ago would have been classified as literature—and poor literature at that. Richardson (2000) describes several literature types, including ethnographic fiction, poetic representation, readers' theater, and autoethnography. Richardson goes as far as to label these new genres of ethnography as *creative analytical practice ethnography,* or *CAP ethnography.* The gist of this new avenue of research includes "new work, future work, and older work, wherever the author has moved outside conventional social scientific writing," which helps "break down the mind/body duality" (Richardson 2000, 9).

Essential to the type of ethnography advocated by Richardson, Denzin, and others is the role the ethnographer plays in producing lived evocative experience expressed through text. It can also be cast in nonwritten forms. This type of representation relates the personal to the cultural and opens up a cast of areas and behavioral niches left untouched or beyond the reach of conventional ethnography. Living through the body, the ethnographer can access feelings, ambiguities, temporal sequences, blurred experiences, and other aspects not uncovered through participant observation. In this evocative textual form, a narrative or ethnographer's story, the ethnographer loses the need to deal with the tension of self and other as the ethnographer becomes other. To put it bluntly, the medium becomes the message. "Casting social science into evocative forms reveals the rhetoric and the underlying labor of the production as well as social science's potential as human endeavor because evocative writing touches us where we live, in our bodies" (Richardson 2000, 11).

Earlier, chapter 6 explored postmodern ethnography in relation to a humanistic positivism. In this chapter, some of the same kinds of ethnographic tools—narrative, self-reflexivity, self-dissolving into other—are used in producing an experiential ethnography in which the ethnographer actively and intensely participates in the culture as one of its members. Instead of writing a narrative that focuses on the relationship of experience to the ethnographer, the fieldworker attempts to access the cultural reality of all cultural members, not only through his or her experiences but also through canvassing other cultural members. Studying sport offers the athletically skilled ethnographer, if inclined to compete or perform with the athletes, an opportunity to become a participating member of the sport population.

This chapter will explore the nature of sport ethnography when the fieldworker becomes a participating member of the culture. I have labeled this *experiential ethnography* (Sands 1991, 1995, 1999c, 1999d) and have suggested elsewhere that fieldwork is accomplished through complete immersion over a long period (see chapter 3). In this journey the ethnographer travels through a series of doors, or stages, just as athletes move through seasons in sport. Each door provides a deeper understanding of the culture and behavior of the population. Unlocking each door and gaining the code to decipher cultural behavior takes on the trappings of a rite of passage, whether subtle or overt, directly or indirectly acknowledged by both ethnographer and cultural members. Integral to this type of study is reflexivity and narrative, whereby the ethnographer becomes just another informant providing information and experiences to the understanding of the culture. The ethnographer's experience is not the central focus of the ethnography. Instead, it validates the experience and behavior of many or most cultural members.

This chapter will discuss several key points:

- Complete participation
- Unlocking doors of experience and rites of passage
- Sensuous ethnography
- Reflexivity, narrative, and experience

Complete Participation

As discussed earlier, traditional ethnography was an uneasy alliance between observation and passive participation. Believing that successful ethnography demanded an objectivity and occupational distancing of ethnographer from cultural members, fieldwork was characterized by the invisible observer, always watching, occasionally taking part in cultural and social intercourse, but never losing the role of scientist. The ethnographer was always the cultural infant, mediating a chasm between wannabe cultural member and cultural annotator. For Geertz, this produced a natural tension between cultural members and ethnographer and even between the different roles experienced by the ethnographer. This cultural member–ethnographer dichotomy was portrayed earlier as self versus other. It has become obvious in the era of new or interpretive ethnography (most recently postmodernism), however, that there is a similar conflict of insider versus outsider that plays within the mind of the ethnographer and is expressed in the ethnographer's cultural experiences. In other words, the ethnographer is living testimony to one level of self versus other. Those in the culture cast the ethnographer in the role of outsider, and this dichotomy, at least initially for many, is necessary for fieldwork to succeed. On the other hand, the ethnographer experiences the same dichotomy internally when he or she is not absorbing knowledge or meaning.

One way of getting around or through this natural tension is to plant both ethnographic feet firmly in the role of outsider. By anchoring to a role acknowledged by both ethnographer and cultural member as discrete and distinct, complicity or duplicity does not exist on the part of the ethnographer toward cultural members. Outside will never be inside—this is a postmodern ethnographic strategy. The second method is to go to the other extreme by becoming an insider, to participate and have similar cultural experiences as other athletes or cultural members.

Belinda Wheaton spent a great deal of time windsurfing the waves off English beaches—not just windsurfing but hanging around on cold, wet beaches, in pubs that the windsurfers frequented, on road trips around the U.K. coastline and beyond, in windsurfing shops and car boot sales—so that she could experience the culture and become another windsurfer. Anne Bolin, following Alan Klein's ethnography of bodybuilders, is more than an occasional participant in the gym and continues to compete in bodybuilding to understand the cultural ramifications of not only the competition but also the cultural perception of the body. Jane Granskog competes as a masters' triathlete, and Susan Brownell spent a full season as a competing member (heptathlete) of a Chinese women's collegiate track team. Granskog's study focused on the effect of the triathlon culture on her personality and perception of cultural behavior, whereas Brownell's study focused on the role of the body in empowering Chinese female athletes and women. My work has resulted in complete participation as a basketball player, collegiate sprinter, collegiate football player, and now surfer.

In each of these cases, participation was an avenue to glean in-depth, representative data of a culture. In some cases, the ethnographer reflected on personal experiences in the narrative, but he or she was not the focus of fieldwork; the narrative was more a conduit to eventual reconstruction of cultural reality.

The sidebar summarizes the key components of what I have labeled *experiential ethnography*.

Components of Experiential Ethnography

1. The researcher participates as one of the population in every aspect of his or her interaction.

2. The researcher must travel through numerous layers of participation, from passive observation and participation (at the outset) to extensive participation and becoming one of the population (see Keesing 1979 and Lehman 1985 for a more complete discussion of cognitive and behavioral levels of understanding).

3. The stay in the field is for a lengthy period, giving the researcher control over social fluctuations in interaction that occur infrequently and allowing a more stable and complete picture of the population to emerge (see Ellen 1984, Sanjek 1990, Stocking 1983, Foster et al. 1979, Smith and Kornblum 1989, and Kottack 1983).

4. Observation becomes integrated within the participation—in other words, intensive participation is at once participation and observation.

5. Interaction forms an important part of validation (this suggests adherence to the competence theory of cognitive science).

The ethnographer acquires data in the same way that any new cultural member would gain the necessary behaviors for becoming a cultural member. This process allows the ethnographer access to deeper levels of meaning pertinent to the culture through deeper levels of experience. For all practical purposes, the ethnographer learns how to become an athlete in that culture, through physical skills and acceptable behavior.

In the case of Wheaton, already a windsurfer, the problems associated with experiential methodology centered around being able to fit the role of fieldworker into the experience, unlike the usual problem of being accepted in the culture. In this type of research in performance-based sport, participating and performing to the level of other cultural members is paramount. In all my research, a great deal of acceptance and interaction was based on cultural scenes that occurred in gyms, on fields, and on tracks. Not being able to play football, compete at the track meets, or be picked for recreation pickup basketball games would have rendered my fieldwork one-dimensional and devoid of much explanatory power. More to the point, complete participation became a ticket into the nexus of interaction between group members, both competitive and social. Becoming an integral part of this interaction became a means of gaining access to knowledge as well as allowing the incorporation and transfer of knowledge.

Going Native: The Duality of Roles

Complete participation has led in some cases to an extreme orientation of the ethnographer toward the culture and cultural members. Referred to as *going native*, the ethnographer becomes immersed to the point that he or she loses the cultural background brought into the field and aligns with the worldview of the culture studied. This integration is so complete that the ethnographer "defends and romanticizes their values" (Wheaton 1997) while losing detachment to the spirit of ethnography. In ethnography of non-Western cultures, the ethnographer becomes sympathetic to the plight of the cultural members and in some cases chooses the life of the native over the former identity.

Experiential ethnography only takes the idea of going native to the extent of complete immersion. An experiential ethnography maintains ethnographic method and research goals. Examples of experiential or complete sport ethnography in this book include the work of Klein, Bolin, Wheaton, and Brownell, because they became whom they were studying by taking on the experience, behavior, and cultural mind-set of cultural members. I suggest that it is almost impossible not to adopt the identity of athlete after engaging in the long-term commitment required by fieldwork. In fact, I suggest that this type of ethnography can only be successful if the ethnographer intuitively knows through acceptance by cultural members and performance that he or she has become part of the culture. This acceptance and performance becomes part of an overall theory of competence first suggested by the early ethnoscientists Ward Goodenough and Roger Keesing. To them, in the system of language and ultimately culture, one has experienced cultural reality if he or she is able to perform linguistically and culturally like a native, passing the muster of cultural members.

Labeling his work as that of a "relative insider," Giulianotti eschewed any identification as a native and kept his personal, professional, and ethical distance from the two football clubs he studied. His identity during fieldwork was caught between academic and cultural member, but he believes he experienced what other members felt, though in a reduced role. Hughson (1998) suggests that Giulianotti bends to their feelings because he is, after all, human. Armstrong labeled his position vis-à-vis the natives as "marginal native," and he felt that his potential physical violence was not a telling indication of going native but an example of a researcher prone to physical violence in the recreational context of football fan support. Hughson sees Armstrong's position as similar to that of a researcher who enjoys drinking beers and consumes a few beers while conducting research on a pub culture. To both Armstrong and Giulianotti, the only major difference between them and their informants was education—they fit in almost every other way. Yet to both, the distance they were able to sustain helped produce a somewhat realist view of the culture.

The ethnographer can also claim success by undergoing the cognitive tension of maintaining the distinction of fieldworker and cultural member, outsider and insider. When neither fought nor accepted, the tension is a sign that the desired effect of immersion is working. Yet from the standpoint of experiential ethnography, the question remains whether this tension prevents immersion to the point where cultural reality and experience is cognitively duplicated.

If the goal of going native is to achieve a sympathetic, worldview change, the answer is all too obvious—tension is lost as the ethnographer succumbs to the present. But if the goal is to experience the culture with the intent to use fieldwork as a means of description and explanation, tension is both a reminder of long-term goals and a means of producing those goals in the form of fieldwork and its eventual text, be it written, film, or other means of presentation.

Bolin and Granskog, Wheaton, and I argue that the success of a performance-based experiential ethnography is predicated on completing an extended period of fieldwork. After the initial period of adjustment by both the ethnographer and cultural members, and as the ethnographer becomes more accepted as part of the cultural scene and social interaction, the fieldworker's ability to fill the roles of participant and cultural analyst becomes more possible. It is less a question of whether it can be done and more a question of discipline and patience. If the ethnographer has the patience, fortitude, and funds to survive and complete two or more years of fieldwork, it is obvious that he or she can organize and spend the time necessary to remove or detach the mind from fieldwork to produce analysis of daily interaction. In my research with college sprinters, I wrote of this duality of roles.

> At night I write of my experience as a sprinter. I invite the anthropologist in me to hold court over my experiences and help me search for meaning in patterns that I am a part of. I invite the scientist in me because he was not there earlier when I ran myself into exhaustion and threw up on the infield. He was not along when I felt the elation of victory and the pain of defeat. I did not ask him to come along with me earlier because there was not room for him inside. At night, I carry out an internal dialogue—sprinter and anthropologist—sorting, classifying, and finally describing the life in the day of a sprinter. This leads to the locating and situating of knowledge naturally. (1995, 9)

In a sense, an ethnographer may be seen as doing an ethnography of himself or herself, but to the extent that the ethnographer is also a representative or informed subject of the culture, a personal ethnography becomes just another voice in the culture.

Time also allows the ethnographer entry to all facets of the experience of the athlete. Athletes, from elite to novice, are framed in cycles of participation. Most cycles follow a preseason, season, and postseason timeline, embedded with seasonal minicycles of intense and less intense behavior. Whatever the sport, the athlete will always complete a cycle and begin another in a somewhat regular or formalized manner. An ethnographer-athlete will need to experience these differing cycles and levels of intensity and commitment.

The ability to switch back and forth between roles and experience is neither novel nor unique to ethnography. Daily, we as humans are role switching and role playing. In the middle of this social milieu, we are able to reason cognitively and analyze our experiences and behavior from different perspectives. Having that ability, the ethnographer is capable of both experience and analysis of experience, even in an intensive experience like experiential ethnography.

Unlocking Doors of Experience

In past work, (1999c, 1999d, and n.d.), I have suggested that the fieldwork experience in a performance-based experiential ethnography is analogous to the ethnographer passing through a series of stages or doors, each of which represents passage to deeper understanding of cultural experience and reality. As the ethnographer opens each door and passes through it, prior experiences act in concert with present experiences to form a more complete understanding of the culture, which in turn guides the ethnographer's path into deeper levels. Cultural members and ethnographer intuitively know or learn about these doors, and they act on the doors socially and culturally. In a loose way, the doors can be thought of as rites of passage—not as sacred, life-altering rites (as they are defined in anthropology), but as a means of validating and celebrating the cultural experience. The passage through cultural experience and acceptance is not unique to the ethnographer. All cultural members progress through the same passages, undergoing similar rites of passage. That should be no surprise, as the goal of experiential ethnography is to undergo the same cultural experiences that all cultural members do.

In my experiences, some rites were socially and publicly celebrated, whereas others were acknowledged privately. In sport-related fieldwork, rites were often linked to physical prowess and demonstrated skills. In football and track and field, rites were often based in a measure of masculinity or manhood. My first football practice, my first hit, my first injury, my first game, my first selection as captain, my first start, my first completion, my first after-game party—all were examples of publicly acknowledged rites of passage.

Bolin and Granskog, in a paper given at the 1999 NASSS meetings entitled "Going Native, Going Anthropologist: When You Are Who You Study," suggest a similar rite-of-passage experience for the experiential ethnographer. Using Guedon's experiences with Dene women, in which being a woman was not a biological fact as much as it was a process or act of participation (Guedon 1994, 43), Bolin and Granskog see participant observation as a process of the ethnographer's maturing into the culture, supported by cultural members, the Dene in this case. "This has clear resonance for ethnographers of sport, whose own sport experience involves them in a rite of passage as they progress in knowledge of the athletic endeavor as time and experience accumulate" (Bolin and Granskog, n.d.).

Hidden Dimensions Revealed

Any type of performance-based ethnography, or experiential ethnography, is situated not only in the cognitive or idealist and learned and shared spheres of culture but also in a more sensuous, bodily, or kinesthetic experience of the performance, whether it be sport, theater, or dance. Because they go through the process of unlocking doors and experiencing rites of passage, performance ethnographers are poised to access this sphere of body-intense activity because they have experienced the same somatic and kinesthetic experience.

In my research with sprinters and football players, I experienced sensations and feelings through participation that would have lain outside the nonexperiential ethnographer's boundaries of observation. In effect, my body's lived experience of performance and competition not only allowed me access to sensations of pain, elation, adrenaline rushes, and wild swings of emotion generated through cognitive appraisal of performance but also brought me closer to the cultural experiences of my teammates and other like athletes.

Sport is as much an activity of the body as it is of the mind. Much of the physical experience of sport lies rooted in what de Garis (1999) labels the *sensuous*. To most people, the word *sensuous* has a sexual overtone, but de Garis uses it to describe the feelings pertaining to the senses. As any athlete knows, much of participation and competition cannot be translated through sight or verbally communicated to others, especially nonathletes. Despite being unable to communicate this realm of experience through the more traditional means of interviews, observations, and field notes, de Garis suggests that sport ethnography, or what I call experiential ethnography, brings to the field of investigation an opportunity to develop a methodology that makes lived experience real to others' perception of sport experience.

In his pro-wrestling career, de Garis was a subject of an ethnography authored by nonwrestler Sharon Mazur. In the eyes of de Garis, her unwillingness to participate in the experiential part of wrestling limited her ability to tap into performative aspects of wrestling that lay outside the scope of the visual: ". . . sensuous knowledge are extremely meaningful kinds of data that are unattainable for those who rely on visual observation" (1999, 71). For example, in a physical sport like wrestling, a gentle and light touch is desired, and one responds to queries about performance by describing the feel or the feeling as "light, strong, gentle, rough" (1999, 72).

A Sensuous Example: No Pain, No Gain

Like de Garis, I found myself keyed in to the arena of somatic and sensuous in my research with sprinters and football players. In sprinting, the pain of competition is anaerobic-based and brought on by oxygen deprivation to muscles. It is a much different pain than that experienced by long-distance runners. Yet, for each activity, the lived experience of pain is both necessary and a barometer to success. Once someone has literally sprinted into this state of pain and experienced the toll it takes on the body and mind, its effects can be more easily understood. To experience it only once or infrequently, however, begs the effect that this kind of pain has on the body and mind when repeatedly, and voluntarily, experienced. Thus, pain becomes a state that is not the end all, but just a step to a much larger

University of Illinois sprinter Lee Bridges experiences the "sensuous" of sprinting. To him, as well as me, pain was a friend.

experience, that of attaining goals. Somehow distancing the mind from the effect of pain on the body is crucial to sprinting through pain. In a narrative section from my dissertation (1991), reproduced in my book on my research (1995), I write of pain and the need for distancing mind and body. Below is part of that narrative.

The Pain of a Workout

All sprinters who compete have to live with pain. It is constantly there, a companion, an old friend who never dies. You can attempt to ignore it (which you cannot) or fight it (which takes more energy than you have) or live with it. One gets to know pain, dealing with it on your own terms, not its. This may sound too simplistic, but one overcomes pain by simply running through it. This takes mental preparation and an inner strength. Some choose never to acknowledge pain, but it shows on their face in the last 100 meters of a 400-meter race. Then there are those like me who acknowledge pain, maybe include it in conversation, and accept it for what it is—a necessary element just like the weather, the track, the wind and other variables that help determine performance.

Funny thing this pain. It is at its greatest after sprinting, when your body has stopped performing and there is nothing left to occupy your mind or your lungs or your legs or the stuff in between that holds you together. So I treat pain like an old friend. I call it names, I make jokes about it. I never leave home without it. Why lie about it. It is here to stay, so invite it in.

Finally, at the end of a workout, one or two repetitions remain—probably the last one. You know damn sure that your body and legs wanted to stop on the previous one, but you also know that these last two sprints are the most important ones of the workout—almost as if all sprints up to this point are acts leading to a grand finale. It is only after this final performance and the curtain falls that one can take a bow. I cannot stall any longer—I toe the line for the last sprint and go. My legs cannot shake off the fatigue and I dig down a little deeper than before, shutting my mind off completely. I run and run, fighting the pain. My legs cannot pump any faster because they weigh a ton and my lungs are bursting for air. Then it is over. The drive shuts down as easily as it came on. I am tired and stumble around catching my breath, somehow pulling my body back to my sweats. I guess in a very real way, it is a ritual or rite of passage—passed through each day, each

(continued)

practice. Practice becomes a worship service for my legs. Within this ritual, my body takes precedent over my mind, or maybe in some ways, mind and body fuse. In any case there is something different driving my body. So in the end, I have survived another practice and in the same breath, I can't wait for the next one. For those few practices where everything seems to click and my legs are strong, I do feel really good. I want more and it is always good to leave when one is not quite satiated. For as many of these good practices, there are those where I have thrown up or lay seemingly forever on the track—waiting for my body to return to normality. Even in this agony, my mind turns on and starts to think about what tomorrow will bring. Finally, I am sitting, just minutes away from standing, thinking of what I accomplished today and I say to myself, "it was an ugly day."

Reprinted, by permission, from R. Sands, 1995, *Instant acceleration: Living in the fast lane,* (Lanham, MD: University Press of America), 35–36.

In stepping from the track onto the football field, I discovered that football pain is indeed a far different state in its lived experience and the cultural expectation of its expression. Yet pain felt in a variety of sports does have its commonalities, such as the mantle of excellence that is placed on those who continually experience pain, somehow overcoming it to perform to their expectations or the expectations of others. The face of pain and its somatic experience, however, act to separate out athletes of different sports, and the management of pain comes to personalize or make up the identity of the athlete. For football players, pain was not only internalized and generated from within but also a result of external factors lying outside the body—blocks, tackles, broken bones, and so on—that were a necessary part of the experience. To distinguish different kinds of pain and the effects of sport pain, lived experience of pain was necessary. The experience included the somatic and kinesthetic experience as well as the cognitive identification and management of pain. To de Garis, Mazur needed to undergo the bodily experience of wrestling and at least begin to track the meaning of experiences not easily translated through observation and interviews. To him, an appreciation of some of the more visceral experiences was a start in the right direction. In this respect, a base level of integrating the experiences of lived body with the mind can produce a more definitive reflection of cultural reality. The case can be made that experiencing a severely pulled hamstring 50 meters into a 200-meter race or a dislocated shoulder at the hands of two head-hunting cornerbacks is not essential to being able to communicate one's somatic or kinesthetic experience or those of other athletes. But at the level of elite or competitive sport, the experience of the somatic and sensuous, such as the many faces of pain, surely adds color and meaning to the experience. In other words, somatic experience of pain is a crucial and defining feature of an athlete. Lived experience of feelings attached to senses beyond sight provides access into untapped and undefined experience, and introduces the opportunity to engage in a positivistic discourse in a new area of cultural experience and behavior. A more representative view of cultural reality can then emerge. In part, that is what ethnography is about—making the product more real.

Narrative and Reflexivity in Experiential Ethnography

It is not a coincidence that one of the only ways available to ethnographers to access this realm of somatic and kinesthetic is through the postmodern methodology of narrative. In a postmodern sense, narrative acts to make the cultural experience both real and revealing to the ethnographer. In the arsenal of ethnographic methods, narrative captures the important element of the interaction of ethnographer with cultural members. Making cultural reality real to readers by using the lived experiences of the ethnographer is more than a useful tool—it completes the presentation of research. In that sense, how narrative is formulated and presented becomes just as important as the content. Implicitly and overtly running through this book has been the concept that ethnography can describe and explain cultural reality. Whether the ethnographer or the reader accepts positivism as a meaningful goal of qualitative research does not make narrative any less powerful. Searching for patterns of behavior that shape cultural reality becomes more visible and understood through narrative, especially one informed through self-reflexivity.

For instance, as shown through the example of pain, sport behavior is partially shaped by how pain is perceived and managed by athletes. Reflexive narrative allows access to this phenomenon through a channel not available to the outsider, the nonparticipant. Does the narrative from my sprint research on pain represent a sterile representation, devoid of any explanatory power beyond the reach of the ethnographer? As briefly discussed, the narrative on pain was extremely revealing in providing a chance to view pain as a common but varied expression of sport behavior. Wheaton's work, which included some narrative, provided a view of the male orientation of a less traditional sport, windsurfing. Like other sports well known in structure and participation, windsurfing expressed similar malecentric characteristics. Lived experience was extremely useful in delineating this malecentrism. In Klein's work on bodybuilders, narrative allowed the cultural scene of the gym to be shown to be similar in many behaviors and characteristics no matter the location. Bolin's work on bodybuilders produced reflexive narrative that was instrumental in expressing how an earlier, more literary attempt at reproducing the culture of female bodybuilders was deficient in uncovering the characteristics of a bodybuilder. Experience, and a reflexive narrative, by itself does not make cultural reality come alive. For this to occur, narrative must be grounded not only in experience but in a systematic attempt to frame this experience in lived representation of both ethnographer and cultural member, supplemented by the use of other tools of ethnography, such as interview, observation, life histories, field notes, and so on.

The value of experiential ethnography can best be put to use deconstructing and then making explainable the cultural behavior of athletes at all levels of performance, all ages, both genders, and all cultural identities. Pressing problems of sport participation, the effect of participation on the athlete off the field, the role of parents in sport socialization, domestic violence and criminal behavior of elite athletes, sport violence, and other social and cultural problems capture headlines and shape our discussions at work and home. As I complete this chapter, the incident of a hockey father beating another to death after their sons' game is front-page news and is portrayed in depth in newspapers and magazines (Nack and Munson 2000). It is one thing to tender statistically based studies and research on these problems—which are neither unique nor uncommon to our society as a whole—and yet to another be able to dissect and offer *experience* as a means for elucidating cultural behavior and defining cultural reality. Experiential knowledge provides us with a more in-depth "partial truth" than has been available in the past.

Painting stereotypes is almost a cultural pastime for many of us. The label *athlete* conjures up various personality and behavior stereotypes. Many of these stereotypes are negative. To peer into these stereotypes and represent them and the cultural reality that produces such behavior is one of the only ways to offer an understanding of behavior. Stereotypes are grounded in ignorance and avoidance. To bring to light nuances of human behavior that heretofore have been cloaked in a shadow of superficial analysis is to help glean the patterns of behavior that make us all human. This is what experiential ethnography offers—a deconstruction of stereotypes and a means to place the flesh of behavior on the skeleton of truth.

Conclusion

Experiential ethnography is not really a novel way of doing sport ethnography. In any kind of ethnography, the fieldworker cannot help but become intertwined with the culture, interactions, and experience. The movements of interpretive and postmodern ethnography legitimized the previously undiscussed variable of cultural experience on the ethnographer and opened up new strategies of accessing cultural experience. To integrate these strategies into ethnography, the stranglehold of empiricism that had driven traditional ethnography had to be lessened. This development created a space for richly textured techniques like reflexive narrative to get at the cultural experience and produce a more accurate map of cultural reality.

In the long run, the question of how far the ethnographer should go in immersion is perhaps best dictated by the research perspective and research context. In other words, why should the flexibility of ethnography not include flexibility when it comes to involvement? In experiential ethnography, the idea of complete immersion may not be possible outside of cultural situations advocating deviant moral stances or issues, such as Giulianotti's and Armstrong's research. Again, as Armstrong, Giulianotti, Wheaton, I, and others have discovered, how far native one should go is a question that only the ethnographer and those intimately involved in the culture can answer.

In any kind of research involving human agents, personality, perception, and even agenda weigh heavily on the outcome and conclusions. This chapter has described a research method in ethnography that uses the ethnographer as an integral part of both the research and experience. Some recent examples of such a method were presented, and suggestions were offered about how future research in experiential ethnography may be applied. As discussed earlier, the nature of sport ethnography presents an exciting opportunity to use the tools of contemporary ethnography, especially reflexive narrative, to study athletes, sport, and sport cultures. In this perspective, sport ethnography sits on the cusp of ethnographic innovation in method and strategy.

Chapter 10

Ethnography for Hire

> *As an ethnographic research and consulting firm that employs a proprietary database of over 1,700 cultural anthropologists located around the world, Context has the global reach and insider knowledge to translate consumer behavior into powerful business strategy. Context Research delivers ethnography at the speed of business.*
>
> —Context-Based Research Group (**www.contextresearch.com**)

In the last decade, ethnography has been discovered as an important tool for use in the marketplace. Business and management faculties at colleges and universities have borrowed the concept of culture and applied it to large and small businesses. The culture concept applies not only to the interactions of management and staff but also to the shared and learned qualities of ideas and traditions that circulate throughout the business. Businesses that strive to maintain open lines of communication and cultivate a voice for the employees—when it comes to suggestions and ideas for improvement—will succeed and present a positive image for the public and consumers. Public approval translates into public spending.

When hired to come in and fix mismanaged businesses, management consultants use ethnographic methodology in describing a company's cultural reality. Included in the "softer" side of management intervention, consultants deal with organizational dynamics, change management, organizational behavior, group facilitation, and so on. The concepts of cultural holism and integration, when applied to the business culture, make it fruitful for the consultants to take a participant-observation strategy into company fieldwork and piece together the structural relations from the inside. Yet, in some ways, consulting involves some striking departures from traditional or academic ethnography. Alan Hinsey, the president of Management Intervention Services, views his work as a mission impossible: "We come in from the outside, quickly diagnose the problem, make recommendations and assist with corrective action, then we leave as quickly as we came" (personal communication, July 4, 2000). Hinsey is never perceived as an insider, one who experiences the organization's cultural reality, nor is there any effort to seduce those in the company into believing that he is. To Hinsey, like most ethnographers, cultural reality is mostly derived from the cultural members. "I am no smarter that anyone in their organization," said Hinsey. "In fact, all the answers that I will come up with will come directly from their staff people." Hinsey's approach differs from a traditional ethnography in a few important ways. First, it is a task-oriented research method in which the consultant focuses solely on one facet, or to Hinsey, one problem at a time (or at least it appears that way to the client). Second, consultants are paid to solve the problem of cultural malfunctioning. Finally, unlike the fieldworker in traditional ethnography, the consultant does not work or live in the corporate culture. As a result, outsider status is reified, allowing the consultant to ask difficult or imposing questions that cultural members would find intrusive if asked by insiders.

Ethnography is also useful in exploring the relationship of product and consumer. To succeed in today's niche-oriented world, businesses must "culture-test" their products to make sure that the product and the buyer match up. Knowing the cultural reality of the buyer is imperative for designing the product to fit cultural members' needs and for planning advertising campaigns that effectively alert the cultural consumer to the product's selling points. Qualitative research methods used in business include focus groups, point-of-purchase interviewing, phone interviewing, and questionnaires. But many companies have realized that ethnography offers a more in-depth look at the needs and wants of cultural members. Cultural members' reality provides a framework for building successful market strategy.

Government groups have also recognized the value of ethnography. For the 2000 United States census, the Census Bureau recruited ethnographers to propose and carry out fieldwork to determine household size, family membership, and composition of nontraditional families living in the United States. Ethnographers were also recruited to do similar studies with homeless and indigent Americans to assist in the census count.

Sport is big business in Western societies and has become an integral part of the global economy. For this reason, sport is ripe for employing ethnographic techniques. The National Football League and the National Basketball Association are on an evangelistic quest to make their products globally successful. The World Football League plays in Europe, professional basketball leagues operate in many countries across the globe, and last year the Cubs and the Mets opened the major-league baseball season with a game in Japan. To sell the sport, the NFL and NBA must search for cultural traits or trends of the prospective host country. For example, the NFL must look at Barcelona, Spain, to present the commodity of football, its WFL, to the inhabitants. Each sport may refer to itself as the world's greatest game, yet Klein's work on Latin baseball and Whiting's work on Japanese baseball, along with a plethora of offerings from Hollywood, have shown that baseball has indeed become the sport of choice for most of the planet.

Sport connects with participants not only through the experience but also through equipment, apparel, and footwear. Professional teams arouse the imagination and whet the appetite for mere mortals to experience the same rush of competition as the gods of professional sports do, if on a lower level of ability. Sport has also become a hot commodity on the Internet as the number of on-line businesses explodes in search of markets. The Internet is the home for fantasy sports, allowing participation in America's pastimes to take place at the touch of a computer keyboard (see a later section for an example of business ethnography done on this phenomenon).

Several labels are used to identify ethnographers in business—cultural researcher, cultural consultant, cognitive designer, information specialist, analyst—the list goes on. What each label defines is a role that uses the tools of ethnography discussed in this book—participation, observation, interviews, life histories, and so on. The only real difference between traditional ethnography and ethnography for hire is that the ethnography in the marketplace travels at the light speed of business. Businesses live and die on the fickleness of the consumer, and the timely identification and implementation of marketing strategy is crucial to success. Dot-com companies have changed the face of marketing. Information and data on buyers must be available yesterday. Long-term fieldwork is measured in weeks, even days. The ethnographer must press fieldwork to fit this need. Field reports and final statements of findings, in effect, the business ethnography, are turned around at a clip that would make even the most passionate fieldworker blanch in despair. This method seems to contradict the canon of long-term fieldwork presented in this book. But the superficial nature of market ethnography, the shotgun approach, and the specificity of topic preclude the holistic, in-depth nature of academic ethnography.

This chapter offers examples of cultural research done outside the sometimes imposing, rigid walls of the ivory tower. The irony of the progressiveness and liberal nature of academia being juxtaposed against the inherent conservatism of the machinations of academia is not lost on me. When the shackles of a certain approach (i.e., postmodernism or positivism) are discarded—business rarely cares about labels or their meaning, just about results—the business study becomes an amalgamation of strategies and methods that simply retrieve the kind and amount of data and information needed. The following three studies will describe the process as it relates to the nature of the business of sport.

Rackets

In the summer of 1994 I was approached by John Lowe, president of Cultural Analysis, Inc., about doing ethnographic research for an account from a public relations firm he had just received concerning Wilson Sporting Goods. Concerned about the perception of the buyer when it came to the label, the company wanted to understand what products the public associated with Wilson and what images or symbols were conjured up when Wilson was displayed or communicated. I was contracted to do a study with a turnaround of three weeks. I needed to locate and interview six subjects who were sports minded and within a certain age range. Methodology was simple and direct. On playing fields, tennis courts, tracks, and beach volleyball courts (considering the locale of Santa Barbara, California), I would participate in games, make some kind of connection with the players, and when the games were over, offer a fee if they would sit down for a 90-minute taped, opened-ended interview at their home.

Sampling from a crazed two-week period of nonstop pickup games, tennis matches, and beach volleyball games produced six interviewees—three male and three female, ranging in age from 16 to 40. Working from a list of 10 prepared questions, including biographical information on each participant, a perceptual image of Wilson Sporting Goods emerged. Attributes like tradition, trustworthiness, and quality were applied to Wilson. At the same time, these attributes worked against Wilson when innovation, creativity, and trend setting were applied to the label. Sport was an important vehicle for the marketing of Wilson's production line. In a way, Wilson was looking to expand across cultures of sport and discover the meaning and worth of the label *Wilson* in an expanding sports equipment and apparel market.

After listening to the nine hours of taped interviews and completing the field notes, I began to analyze the data. Within a week I had completed the report. John then did his own interviews. He submitted a written analysis of the field data and interviews to the ad agency handling the Wilson campaign a week later. From start to finish we completed the project in under a month. Unable to allow the fieldwork to proceed at the pace of natural social intercourse and experience, the ethnographer must force the pace of fieldwork to match the deadline of the contract. In this case, the short time frame did not allow any shared experience between subjects and me, other than the brief period of participation I spent identifying prospective interviewees. My past experiences in sports, however, were shared by informants and provided an important foundation on which to initiate fieldwork.

Beer

In the summer of 1995, just as I finished teaching a summer school class and sweating through summer football drills, John again contracted me to take part in a study for an advertising company that represented Heineken Beer. The study was an effort to understand how Heineken Beer fit into two key target segments, males age 21 to 24 and an older group of premium beer drinkers, age 25 to 35 of both genders. Fieldwork involved in-home interviews, a night of barhopping with each interviewee, and observation of premium beer drinking to get at the symbolic meaning of Heineken in the culture and how it influences behavior. The two fieldwork methods, interview and observation, acted to inform us about the meaning of the label and beer and to understand the beer drinkers themselves—what matters to them, what a product means, and then how they integrate that product or symbol into their daily lives. I selected informants from a group of contacts given to me by friends and acquaintances and from chance meetings in Santa Barbara locations. As before, the interviews were 90 minutes long and open-ended, producing an in-depth look at the personal space and cultural items that reflected personal taste and buying habits, both important to Heineken for understanding the purchasing motivations of potential customers.

Questions were designed to

- identify the respondents through brand choice, habits, personae, and values that undergird behavior;
- discover the motivation and symbolization that went into the selection of a beer;
- determine what part beer plays in the respondents' lives and in comparison with other alcoholic beverages;
- uncover rituals that define usage and lead to expectations of companionship and establishment of mood in conjunction with beer drinking;
- decode how Heineken is perceived, its cultural meaning, and its perceived authenticity as a premium beer;
- query informants about how drinking Heineken could be made more compelling.

While John completed his fieldwork in Manhattan, I concentrated on the West Coast. As I began the fieldwork in early August, I was the envy of my football teammates—most of whom were not old enough to make the cut—and my friends. The contract included expense money for paying the informants for their time and to provide the beer and entertainment during observation. Ten days later, after six evenings spent in observation—barhopping up and down State Street in Santa Barbara—and completing six interviews, I was exhausted and more than a little tired of the green bottles of Heineken. I had killed more than a few brain cells, which I desperately needed to write up the report.

Staring down the barrel of an imposing deadline, I spent 48 hours, with just brief periods of respite and recovery, writing the report, which defined the population, their lifestyles, the cultural perception of beer, and the place of Heineken in the beer market. Half of the report centered on understanding the personalities and lifestyles of the informants. Knowing the market is essential to creating a broad appeal, to satisfying more than just a niche. The remainder of the report was spent discussing the place of beer, specifically Heineken, in the culture of beer drinkers and the market. I found it interesting that all the informants were active in sport and lived a lifestyle that centered on physical activity. Two respondents were professional athletes, in tennis and volleyball. All were extremely conscious of the relationship between body image and success. Over all, the construction and management of image was a defining characteristic of potential success.

My conclusions centered on an ironic conundrum—Heineken was the symbol of premium quality, authenticity, and both social and financial success. Yet in some ways, this limited the appeal of the beer to those who perceived themselves as such. Maintaining a hold on the Cadillac or Porsche nature of this perception while reinventing the label for other markets were seen as crucial goals. After the pressure and work that went into finishing the report, I felt like celebrating and having a beer but instead wisely went to bed.

Cyber Sport

The spring of 2000 produced a chance to be a sport and culture consultant to an advertising company seeking the campaign of a fantasy-sports Web page. In this case, I was not required to do fieldwork or conduct interviews, but was instead used as a resource to help legitimize a presentation to a particular business. Instead of directing research, I was part of someone else's fieldwork!

Contract ethnography has become a hot commodity in the marketplace, and several anthropology-ethnography research firms have formed for just that purpose. As business is becoming a niche-oriented enterprise, consultant-contractors have been in demand for their expertise to furnish in-depth looks at cultural behavior and experience. These ethnography companies are loose consortiums of contract ethnographers who are recruited by companies to do fieldwork in their particular areas of expertise. Because my area of interest is sport and culture, an ethnography company contacted me to act as a consultant to an advertising company that was preparing to pitch an ad campaign to a fantasy-sport Web page.

Ad companies spend much of their time developing potential ad campaigns to solicit clients. In this case, the client was one of the several Internet Web pages that cater to the growing number of fantasy-sport players. Fantasy sport has grown from the rotisserie leagues, in which friends sat around over beers following the day-to-day playing statistics of their favorite baseball players, to a multimillion-dollar enterprise that offers large cash winnings to players. Like many cultural behaviors and experiences, using the Internet has changed the scope of our existence. Players can compete against others from all over the world or form their own league of players with location of the players not a limiting factor. From baseball, fantasy sport has reached out to include football, golf, hockey, and tennis. Some Web pages even offer political campaigns under the umbrella of fantasy sports. Web pages such as Smallworld.com and Sandbox.com cater solely to fantasy sport. Prominent sport Web pages such as ESPN.com and CNNSI.com also provide the opportunity for sport enthusiasts to participate in fantasy sport.

I was contracted to do conference calls with the key personnel in the project, providing them with information and data to help prepare their presentation. Project members on a conference call then videotaped me for two and a half hours answering questions provided. Because I was on the West Coast and they were located in Boston, a video and audio professional from Hollywood drove up and turned my kitchen into a production studio. With a small headphone feeding the conference call into my ear, I provided cultural information on topics of sport and culture that affected perceptions of how to increase the marketability of the Web page. The ad company also shot six hours of what they labeled "Blair Witch Fantasy Baseball." They filmed a group of fantasy players conducting the season-beginning draft by computer with players in Toronto, Canada, and elsewhere.

Fundamental to this marketability is identifying the consumer, "players" in this case, and then tailoring the Web page to attract those consumers. Interesting questions emerged:

- Who played fantasy sport?
- Were they fans, frustrated athletes, Internet stat nerds, pundits, those desiring to be coaches or general managers?
- What were they deriving from their participation? Was money a key component to what fantasy-sport Web page they used?
- Did the Internet limit participation to computer literate, middle- to upper-class professional males?
- Was playing fantasy sport a substitute for athletic experience, or was it one that supplemented sport and recreation experience?
- Did fantasy sport describe an Internet culture—members who shared and learned cultural behavior, complete with tradition, particular language, unique cultural artifacts, and so forth? (See chapter 4 for more on culture.)
- What was the future of fantasy sport? The Internet crosses traditional cultural boundaries and national borders. Would fantasy sport play well outside Western culture? Could fantasy sport attract females as well?

I drew on my ethnographic experience and research, both experiential and literary, to offer pertinent knowledge and in some cases to help frame hypotheses concerning the intersection of sport culture and fantasy sport. The questions listed earlier can apply, with some modification, to the direction of sport in the new millennium. The Internet is fast becoming a cyber playing field, gym, or stadium. As sport reflects culture, so does the Internet.

A Note on the Internet and Ethnography

Ethnography has always been a tool for use in the science of meaning, as much as this meaning has been rooted to context. Cyber sport, to a large extent, rips or melts specific traditional cultural contexts, reducing behavior and experience down to bits of data, which then requires a re-creation of the bits into an understandable context. Yet as the Internet restructures the way we see, use, and react to knowledge, cyber reality is creating a cyber culture that offers, at least to generations of my age and older, a more sterile, less richly textured experience.

Culture acts as a share-and-teach idea to cultural members—what acts to unite members in a culture is the limited number of interpretations of those ideas. Interpretations of ideas, couched in symbols, approach infinity as the ideas are removed from cultural context and programmed into computers. In a cyber culture that instantly crosses cultural boundaries, one interpretation is now as valid as the next. What make us human are both our universality and our differences; to emphasize one over the other destroys the tenuous balance that helped create humanity. One can say that the evolution of the Internet is creating a culture that is just another expression of traditional cultures, similar to how sport and individual sports and athletes have been cast as culture in this book. Yet, as the third millennium introduces new groupings of humans formed around features or traits that are a product of our ride through the roller-coaster technology of today and tomorrow, cultural identity, feelings of being a part of a group, and allegiance are trampled by the self-gain and control of the flow of knowledge of a few. Ethnography can become an unwitting participant in this deconstruction, but in another sense it can help keep us informed of the effects of cyber culture on human behavior. Bohannon and van der Elst see the Internet as a new stage in cultural evolution:

The idea that all of recorded human experience can be accessed and used for anyone's idiosyncratic purpose is exciting on a number of levels, not all of them attractive. . . . all human knowledge is being collected and encoded, while meaning and context are either being ignored or else transformed into art that will alter, inform and change . . . everything." (1999, 90)

Although I am not as dire as Bohannan and van der Elst in their caution, the effects of the Internet on the expression of the culture of sport was clearly seen in the work done on cyber sport. Ethnography has always been and still is a tool for understanding human behavior. Ethnography is now becoming a tool for more than just social scientists and more than just formalized research. It is now more in the hands of what Bohannon and van der Elst call "everyman." The founding discipline of anthropology should not be covetous of its ethnographic turf. Now more than ever, with geographical and social space reduced to the thickness of fiber optics, rubbing elbows with those who have different perspectives of reality can be achieved just as it is by walking down a street in urban America. Culture is a phenomenon now divisible into common interests that tie all humanity together, whereas other facets are common only to a few—not just on culture by culture example, but on a worldwide basis. With drastic culture change occurring with unprecedented rapidity, ethnography becomes a highly useful tool for understanding this culture change. As the new millennium opens up to technological advances that boggle the mind—for example, human genome mapping and cloning—human social and physical interaction will not only carry these new advances but also express the profound effect on our values and beliefs.

A Concluding Word

Ethnography for hire represents the trend toward the use of in-depth cultural research in areas outside academics. Most academicians have at one time or another been accused of existing in the rarefied air of the ivory tower, out of touch with reality. Real-world ethnography produces a brief, focused, and at times superficial look at slices of cultural reality. It lacks the dimension of extended fieldwork and the immersion—the shared, negotiated, or duplicated experience of the ethnographer and cultural member, depending on your theoretical perspective. Ethnography for hire serves those in power who can afford such glimpses of culture. It has become the darling stepchild of capitalism. Yet for all its faults and truncated methodology, ethnography for hire is a means of improving the quality of constantly shifting dialogue of expectations between business and employee, business and consumer, and product and consumer.

Conclusion

Sport is a phenomenon that has come to be a playground—and sometimes a battleground—of different cultures and even for those of the same culture. As true now as it was 64 years ago when the 1936 Summer Olympics was hosted by Germany to trumpet a racial platform of superiority, sports have become an effective way to solidify cultural identity and promote cultural values and lifeways. As the nature of inter- and intracultural interaction has changed dramatically in the last half century, the mechanisms and strategies that guide such interaction have changed as well. Yet what has not changed much is the idea that these mechanisms and strategies are common—and universal—to cultures all over the world. Thus ethnography has become a powerful and necessary enterprise, complete with interviews, observation, and participation to understand how these universals, such as sport, have changed and how they have remained the same.

I write this concluding chapter on June 16, 2000, during a two-week period of terrific late-spring surfing and in the midst of golf's annual U.S. Open. The French Open has just concluded, the Los Angeles Lakers are up three to one over the Indianapolis Pacers in the NBA championships, and rumors fly that Sammy Sosa is on the trading block. The orgasm of international sport, the Summer Olympics, is just two months away. It is a wonder that I can sit long enough to marshal my thoughts and attempt to write a concluding chapter to this book. Even if I wanted to, I could not avoid the high drama of sport.

I come back from my morning surf tired but exhilarated from the waves. Just a few days ago, before leaving on my surf expedition, I had tuned in the live 5 A.M. coverage of the French Open from Roland Garros. Now as I lower my head to look at the keyboard, drops of saltwater drip from my nose onto the keys. I battle the desire to rush into the TV room and watch the second round of the U.S. Open from just up the road at Pebble Beach. I compromise and turn the sound up, hurrying in only at the sound of thunderous roars from the gallery to catch great shots. I get little done but console myself that what I do accomplish is born in the heat of competition. In just a little over an hour, I am due on the tennis court for a match with one of my tennis partners, and when I finish, the fifth game of the NBA series comes on. It won't be till later tonight, after the adrenaline has left me bone tired and I have been overstimulated by all the visceral sport action, that I will sit down for any stretch of time and try to write a few more lines.

This day is no different from any other for me—I cannot get away from the lure and draw of sport, but then again I do not try to. I reflect that I am not abnormal in this fascination. Pick up a newspaper, turn on the television, listen to your friends and acquaintances converse in daily social intercourse—sport and athletes command the most space, air time, or interest. Sport has become, according to Kendall Blanchard, a metaphor for modern life (Blanchard in Sands 1999a). Huge chunks of our daily life telescope into March Madness, Super Bowl frenzy, the Olympics, playoff fever at high school, collegiate, and professional levels, Wimbledon, the Masters— the list is endless, just in the United States. In most other countries, life also revels in the ritual of sport, both Western forms and the indigenous forms that mark a return to traditional ethnicity.

In the beginning of this book, I offered the phrase that "sport reflects culture and culture reflects sport." In essence, sport has become its own culture, broken down into sports and populated by athletes. Its effect on life in the 21st century is dramatic, just as 20th and 21st century life has radically affected sport. Sport is pervasive and never ceasing, casting giant shadows on other facets of life. For a culture, a country, a world to go crazy over a ball game, a camel race, a lacrosse match, a run, speaks volumes about human behavior. Why do we become fanatical over a collection of athletes participating in ritually patterned behavior, repeated over and over down through the ages? What does this say about the nature of human behavior and the personal relationships that reflect this human nature? And perhaps, more germane to the academic world, what does the universal nature of sport in the third millennium say about personal and cultural identity, postmodernism, and the future of the role that sport will play in our lifetime and our children's lifetime?

These questions about today's humanity and other questions that will naturally follow on the footsteps of their answers—you ask questions only so that you can answer more—necessitate research methods that not only reflect the reality of those studied but also propel the researcher into the depths of cultural understanding. It is my belief that ethnography, with all its tools, offers a richly textured view of the culture of sport and the athletes that populate a general and specific cultural reality.

The pace and complexity of life has increased since Malinowski first stepped ashore on a Trobriand island to begin his fieldwork. Of all the measurements that can be brought to bear on the meaning of this pace and complexity, it is ironic that what may be the most complete view of sport, or any other culture or human behavior, is one that is not a traditional view— distant, clinical, or sterile. It is ethnography, in which the author, or scientist (used in a loose meaning), crosses the great divide between objectivity and subjectivity and becomes a living research tool and interpreter.

This book has attempted to bring the canons of ethnography to the quest for meaning of the cultural arena that is today's intricately constructed and symbol-loaded human experience. Innovation and technological advances may range years ahead of knowing the implications and effect of such advances on human behavior presently and in the near future. Taking deep breaths and then submerging into the social chaos and maelstrom of activity, the implications and effect may become more explicit. Player salaries seem to spiral out of control, matching profits from companies. Some even match the gross national product of small countries. On- and off-field behavior of athletes takes them from the heights of the social pedestal into the footsteps of every other mortal, and we wonder why this is so. The importance of sport in Western society is reflected in money earned and spent in pursuit of sport. The global economy and world politics shape and are shaped by the culture of sport. Intercultural interaction is often played out on fields and in gyms, and we wonder whether baseballs and soccer balls can replace diplomacy. Culture changes almost instantaneously. These changes and what they wrought have always been out of our control. Ethnography brings order and understanding out of chaos.

This book is not a step-by-step recipe to do ethnography because there are no definitive ethnographic steps. After a brief summary of anthropology and sport and a nod toward Bronislaw Malinowski and his pioneering efforts, ethnography was defined. Innovation and creativity are just as important as procedure, and the ethnographer must often jury-rig a method. Yet ethnography is accomplished by combining many tools, which were explained and illustrated in individual chapters. Theory plays an important part in determining how these tools are used. Befitting the controversy that rages in the study of human behavior, competing perspectives of postmodernism and positivism were dissected, and I suggested that the perspective of a humanistic science could best help explain human behavior. To this end, I proposed a melding of positivism and interpretation under the guise of an experiential method as an alternative to the autobiographical ethnographer-centrism of postmodern ethnography. Because the value of ethnography has come to be appreciated outside academia, a chapter on the use of ethnography in government and business was presented, supplemented by a note on the power of the Internet.

As the need and desire for ethnography grows, my enthusiasm is tinged with a note of apprehension. Doing good ethnography consists of more than doing some interviewing, observing a game, jotting some notes, even running a 10K road race, and then putting words down on paper. There is much to know about method, interpretation, the role of the ethnographer, the effect on both cultural members and ethnographer, writing good field notes, interviewing styles—the list goes on. Whenever I thought I knew it all, my mother used to remind me that a little bit of knowledge is dangerous. That statement applies here as well. I have discovered that the ethnographer not only must know about the rigors and time intensiveness of ethnography but also must genuinely like people and have compassion for the stories of their personal lives. Because my discipline of anthropology was the birthplace of ethnography and for almost a century has been its safeguard and refiner, I feel somewhat like a father watching his child leave the nest. I am proud of the potential that ethnography offers but hope it will still call home occasionally and ask for guidance. Age and the wisdom of experience still count for much, even in a rapidly changing world. That kind of advice is still free.

Bibliography

Allen, Kerry. 1998. "Mandos Mary." *Surfer's Journal,* 7 (2): 34–37.

Allison, Maria T. and Gunther Luschen. 1979. "A Comparative Analysis of Navajo Indian and Anglo Basketball Sports Systems." *International Review for the Sociology of Sport* 14: 75–86.

Archetti, Eduardo P. 1997. "The Moralities of Argentinian Football." In *The Ethnography of Moralities,* ed. S. Howell. London: Routledge.

Armstrong, G. 1993. "Like That Desmond Morris." In *Interpreting the Field,* ed. D. Hobbs and T. May. Oxford: Oxford University Press.

Aunger, Robert. 1999. "Against Idealism: Contra Consensus." *Current Anthropology* 40: 93–101.

Bale, John, and Joe Sang. 1996. *Kenyan Running: Movement, Culture, Geography and Global Change.* London: Frank Cass.

Barnard, H. 1990. "Bourdieu and Ethnography, Reflexivity, Politics and Praxis." In *An Introduction to the Work of Pierre Bourdieu: The Practice of Theory,* ed. R. Harker, C. Mahar, and C. Wilkes. London: Macmillan.

Bates, Daniel G., and Elliot M. Fratkin. 1999. *Cultural Anthropology,* 2nd ed. Boston: Allyn and Bacon.

Bell, D., P. Caplan, and Jahan Karim, eds. 1993. *Gendered Fields: Women, Men and Ethnography.* London: Routledge.

Bissinger, H.G. 2000. *Friday Night Lights: A Town, a Team, and a Dream.* Cambridge, MA: Da Capo Press.

Blanchard, Kendall. 1981. *The Mississippi Choctaws at Play: The Serious Side of Leisure.* Urbana: University of Illinois Press.

Blanchard, Kendall. 1985. "Sport Studies and the Anthropology of Sport." In *American Sport Culture,* ed. W. Umphlett. Lewisburg, PA: Bucknell University Press.

Blanchard, Kendall. 1995. *The Anthropology of Sport: An Introduction,* 2nd ed. Westport, CT: Bergin and Garvey.

Blanchard, Kendall, and Alyce Cheska. 1985. *The Anthropology of Sport: An Introduction.* Westport, CT: Bergin and Garvey.

Bohannan, Paul, and Dirk van der Elst. 1999. *Asking and Listening.* Mt. Prospect, IL: Waveland Press.

Bolin, Anne, and Jane Granskog. n.d. "Going Native, Going Anthropologist: When You Are Who You Study." Paper presented at the 1999 NASSS meetings, Cleveland.

Bolin, Anne. 1997. "Flex Appeal, Food and Fat." In *Building Bodies,* ed. P. Moore. New Brunswick, NJ: Rutgers University Press.

Bourdieu, Pierre. 1990. *The Logic of Practice.* Cambridge: Polity Press.

Bourgois, Philippe. 1995. *In Search of Respect: Selling Crack in El Barrio.* New York: Cambridge.

Brownell, Susan. 1995. *Training the Body for China: Sports in the Moral Order of the People's Republic.* Chicago: University of Chicago Press.

Brumann, Christopher. 1999. "Writing for Culture: Why a Successful Concept Should Not Be Discarded." *Current Anthropology* 40: 1–25.

Cheska, Alyce Taylor. 1984. "Sport as Ethnic Boundary Maintenance: A Case of the American Indian." *International Review for the Sociology of Sport* 19: 3/4, 241–257.

Culin, Stewart. 1907. "Games of the North American Indians." *Twenty-fourth Annual Report of the Bureau of American Ethnology.* Washington, D.C.: Government Printing Office. Reprinted 1970.

D'Andrade, Roy. 1995. *The Development of Cognitive Anthropology.* Cambridge: Cambridge University Press.

Dandelion, Ben Pink. 1997. "Insider Dealing: Researching Your Own Private World." In *Ethics, Sport and Literature: Crises and Critiques,* ed. Tomlinson and Fleming. Aachen: Meyer and Meyer Verlag.

de Garis, Larry 1999. "Experiments in Pro Wrestling." *Sociology of Sport Journal* 16 (1): 65–74.

Denison, Jim, and Robert Rhinehart. 2000. "Introduction: Imagining Sociological Narratives." *Sociology of Sport Journal* 17 (1): 1–4.

Denzin, Norman. 1997. *Interpretive Ethnography: Ethnographic Practices for the 21st Century.* Thousand Oaks, CA: Sage.

Denzin, Norman, and Yolanda Lincoln. 1998. *The Landscape of Qualitative Research.* Thousand Oaks, CA: Sage.

Durrenburger, Paul. 1999. "Are Ethnographies 'Just So' Stories?" In *Faces of Anthropology,* ed. K. Rafferty and D. Ukaegbu. Needham Heights, MA: Simon and Schuster Custom.

Ellen, Roy F. 1984. *Ethnographic Research: A Guide to General Conduct.* London: Academic Press.

Entine, John. 2000. *Taboo: Why Black Athletes Dominate Sports and Why We Are Afraid to Talk About It.* New York: Public Affairs.

Fine, Gary Alan. 1981. "Preadolescent's Socialization through Organized Athletics: The Construction of Moral Meanings in Little League Baseball." In *Sport in the Sociocultural Process,* ed. M. Hart and S. Birrell. Dubuque, IA: Brown.

Fine, Gary Alan. 1987. *With the Boys: Little League Baseball and Preadolescent Culture.* Chicago: University of Chicago Press.

Firth, Raymond. 1931. "A Dart Match in Tikopia." *Oceania* 1: 64–97.

Foster, George, Elizabeth Colson, Thayer Scudder, and Robert Kemper. 1979. *Long-Term Field Research in Social Anthropology.* New York: Academic Press.

Fox, Robin. 1961. "Pueblo Baseball: A New Use for Old Witchcraft." *Journal of American Folklore* 74: 9–16.

Frake, Charles. 1964. "A Structural Description of Subunum Religious Behavior." In *Explorations in Cultural Anthropology,* ed. W. Goodenough. New York: McGraw-Hill.

Gardiner, Margaret. 1984. *Footprints on Malekula: A Memoir of Bernard Deacon.* Edinburgh: Salamander Press.

Geertz, Clifford, ed. 1973. "Deep Play: Notes on the Balinese Cockfight." In *The Interpretation of Cultures.* New York: Basic Books.

Geertz, Clifford. 1973. *The Interpretation of Cultures.* New York: Basic Books.

Geertz, Clifford. 1983. *Local Knowledge: Further Essays in Interpretive Anthropology.* New York: Basic Books.

Giulianotti, Richard. 1995. "Participant Observation and Research Into Football Hooliganism: Reflections on the Problems of Entree and Everyday Risks." *Sociology of Sport Journal* (12): 1–20.

Gmelch, George. 1972. "Baseball Magic." *Transaction* 8 (8): 39–41.

Goodenough, Ward. 1970. *Description and Comparison in Cultural Anthropology.* Chicago: Aldine.

Griffin, Pat. 1998. *Strong Women, Deep Closets.* Champaign, IL: Human Kinetics.

Granskog, J. 1991. "Tri-ing for Life: The Emergence of the Triathlon Sport Subculture and Its Impact Upon Changing Gender Roles in North American Society." In *Sport . . . The Third Millenium: Proceedings of the International Symposium,* ed. F. Landry. Quebec City, PQ: Presses de l'Universite Laval.

Granskog, J. 1992. "Tri-ing Together: An Exploratory Analysis of the Social Networks of Female and Male Triathletes." *Play and Culture* 5(1): 76–91.

Guedon, Marie Francoise. 1994. "Dene Ways and the Ethnographer's Culture." In *Being Changed by Cross-Cultural Encounters: The Anthropology Extraordinary Experiences,* ed. D. Young and J.-Guy Goulet. Orchard Park, NY: Macmillan.

Hammersley, M., and P. Atkinson. 1995. *Ethnography: Principles in Practice.* London: Routledge.

Hilliard, Dan, 1988. "Finishers, Competitors and Pros: A Description and Speculative Interpretation of the Triathlon Scene," *Play and Culture* 1(4): 300–313.

Hoberman, John. 1997. *Darwin's Athletes.* New York: Houghton Mifflin.

Howell, Nancy. 1990. *Surviving Fieldwork. A Report of the Advisory Panel on Health and Safety in Fieldwork.* Washington, D.C.: American Anthropological Association.

Hughson, John. 1998. "Among the Thugs." *International Review for the Sociology of Sport* 33 (1): 48–57.

Keesing, Roger. 1979. "Linguistic Knowledge and Cultural Knowledge; Some Doubts and Speculations." *American Anthropologist* 81 (1): 12–25.

Keller, J.D., and F.K. Lehman. 1993. "Computational Complexity in the Cognitive Modeling of Cosmological Idea." In *Cognitive Aspects of Religious Symbolism,* ed. P. Boyer. Cambridge: Cambridge University Press.

Klein, Alan. 1988. *Little Big Men: Bodybuilding, Subculture and Gender Construction.* Albany, NY: SUNY Press.

Klein, Alan. 1991. *Sugarball: The American Game, the Dominican Dream.* New Haven, CT: Yale University Press.

Klein, Alan. 1997. *Baseball on the Border.* Princeton, NJ: Princeton University Press.

Kottack, Conrad. 1983. *Assault on Paradise: Social Changes in a Brazilian Field Research Experience.* New York: Praeger.

Kutsche, Paul. 1999. *Field Ethnography.* Upper Saddle River, NJ: Prentice Hall.

Lavenda, Robert, and Emily Schultz. 1999. *Core Concepts in Cultural Anthropology.* Mountain View, CA: Mayfield.

Lehman, F.K. 1985. "Cognition and Computation." In *Directions in Cognitive Anthropology,* ed. J. Dougherty. Urbana: University of Illinois Press.

Lehman, F.K. In press. "Essay #14, Notes on Logical Form in an Intensionalist Semantics." In *Cognitive Science Research Notes.*

Lehman, F.K., and Robert R. Sands. In press. "The Nature of Social Identity and Identity Relationships." In *Lectures on Anthropological Theory.*

Lesser, Alexander. 1933. "The Pawnees Ghost Dance Hand Game: A Study of Cultural Change." In *Columbia University Contribution to Anthropology 16.* New York: Columbia University Press.

Malinowski, Bronislaw. 1922 (1984 reprint). *Argonauts of the Western Pacific.* Mt. Prospect, IL: Waveland Press.

Malinowski, Bronislaw. 1988. *A Diary in the Strict Sense of the Term.* Stanford, CA: Stanford University Press.

Marcus, George. 1999. *Through Thick and Thin.* Princeton, NJ: Princeton University Press.

Marcus, George, and Michael Fisher. 1996. *Anthropology as Cultural Critique.* Chicago: University of Chicago Press.

Mazer, Sharon. In press. "Watching Wrestling–Writing Performance." In *Hop on Pop: The Politics and Pleasures of Popular Culture,* ed. H. Jenkins, T. McPherson, and J. Shattuc. Durham, NC: Duke University Press.

Miller, Barbara. 1999. *Cultural Anthropology.* Boston: Allyn & Bacon.

Miller, Toby. 1997. "The Oblivion of the Sociology of Sport." *Journal of Sport and Social Issues* 21 (2): 115–119.

Nabokov, Peter. 1981. *Indian Running.* Santa Fe, NM: Ancient City Press.

Nack, William, and Lester Manson. 2000. "Out of Control." *Sports Illustrated* 93 (4): 85.

Narby, Jeremy. 1998. *The Cosmic Serpent: DNA and the Origins of Knowledge.* New York: Putnam.

Nash, Dennison. 1999. *A Little Anthropology.* Upper Saddle River, NJ: Prentice Hall.

Nelson, Mariah Burton. 1994. *The Stronger Women Get, the More Men Love Football: Sexism and the American Culture of Sport.* New York: Random House.

Ness, Sally Ann. 1999. "Understanding Cultural Performance: Trobriand Cricket." In *Anthropology, Sport and Culture,* ed. R. Sands. Westport, CT: Bergin and Garvey.

Peacock, James. 1996. "The Future of Anthropology." *American Anthropologist* 99 (1): 9–21.

Plimpton, George. 1966 (1969 reprint). *Paper Lion.* New York: Harper and Row.

Peoples, J., and G. Baily. 2000. *Humanity.* Belmont, CA: Wadsworth.

Radin, Paul. 1920 (1963 reprint). *The Autobiography of a Winnebago Indian.* New York: Dover.

Richardson, Laurel. 2000. "New Writing Practices in Qualitative Research." *Sociology of Sport Journal* 17 (1): 5–20.

Roberts, John, Malcom J. Arth, and Robert R. Bush. 1959. "Games in Culture." *American Anthropologist* 61: 597.

Rose, Dan. 1987. *Black Philadelphia Street Life.* Philadelphia: University of Pennsylvania Press.

Salter, Michael. 1974. "Play: A Medium of Cultural Stability." In *Proceedings from the Third Canadian Symposium on History and Physical Education,* ed. L. Young. Halifax, Nova Scotia.

Sands, Robert R. 1986. "Environmental Factors That Affect Black and White Basketball Performance and Style." Master's thesis, Iowa State University.

Sands, Robert R.1991. "An Ethnography of Black Collegiate Sprinters: A Formal Model of Cultural Identity and the Identity Complex." PhD diss., University of Illinois, Urbana-Champaign.

Sands, Robert R.1995. *Instant Acceleration: Living in the Fast Lane.* Lanham, MD: University Press of America.

Sands, Robert R., ed. 1999a. *Anthropology, Sport and Culture.* Westport, CT: Bergin and Garvey.

Sands, Robert R. 1999b. "Introduction." In *Anthropology, Sport and Culture,* ed. R. Sands. Westport, CT: Bergin and Garvey.

Sands, Robert R.1999c. "Experiential Ethnography: Playing With the Boys. In *Anthropology, Sport and Culture,* ed. R. Sands. Westport, CT: Bergin and Garvey.

Sands, Robert R. 1999d. *Sport and Culture: At Play in the Fields of Anthropology.* New York: Simon and Schuster.

Sands, Robert R.1999e. *GutCheck! A Wild Ride Into the Heart of College Football.* Carpinteria, CA: Rincon Hill Books.

Sands, Robert R. n.d. "Sport Ethnography: Anthropologist as Athlete. Science in a Postmodern World." Unpublished.

Sanjek, Roger. 1990. *Fieldnotes.* Ithaca, NY: Cornell University Press.

Shokeid, M. 1997. "Negotiating Multiple Viewpoints: The Cook, the Native, the Publisher and the Ethnographic Text." *Current Anthropology* 38 (4): 631–45.

Silk, Michael. 1999. "Reconstructing Meanings: The Media Reproduction of Kuala Lumpur 98." PhD diss., University of Otago, New Zealand.

Smith, Carolyn, and William Kornblum. 1989. *In the Field: Readings on the Field Research Experience.* New York: Praeger.

Sparkes, Andrew. 2000. "Autoethnography and Narratives of Self: A Narrative Exploration of Identity in High Performance Sport." *Sociology of Sport Journal* 17 (1): 21–43.

Spradley, James, and David McCurdy. 1980. *The Cultural Experience: Ethnography in Complex Society.* Chicago: Science Research Associates.

Stocking, George. 1983. *Observers Observed.* Madison: University of Wisconsin Press.

Sugdon, John. 1997. "Fieldworkers Rush In (Where Theorists Fear to Tread)." In *Ethics, Sport and Leisure: Crises and Critiques,* ed. Tomlinson and Fleming. Aachen: Meyer and Meyer Verlag.

Telander, Rick. 1976 (1988 reprint). *Heaven Is a Playground.* New York: Simon & Schuster.

Thompson, Hunter. 1972. *Fear and Loathing in Las Vegas.* New York: Random House.

Thompson, Hunter. 1973. *Fear and Loathing on the 1972 Campaign Trail.* New York: Straight Arrow Books.

Tierney, Patrick. 2000. *Darkness in El Dorado: How Scientists and Journalists Devastated the Amazon.* New York: Norton.

Tomlinson, Alan. 1997. "Flattery and Betrayal: Observations on Qualitative and Oral Sources." In *Ethics, Sport and Leisure: Crises and Critiques,* ed. Tomlinson and Fleming. Aachen: Meyer and Meyer Verlag.

Tylor, E.B. 1871. *Primitive Culture.* London: Murrary.

Tylor, Edward B. 1879. "The History of Games." *The Fortnightly Review.* London: Chapman and Hall, 25, n.s. (Jan. 1–June 1): 735–47.

Taylor, E.B. 1896. "On American Lot-Games, As Evidence of Asiatic Intercourse Before the Time of Columbus." *International Archives of Ethnology,* 9: 55–67.

van Maanen, John. 1988. *Tales of the Field: On Writing Ethnography.* Chicago: University of Chicago Press.

Weule, Von Karl. 1925. Ethnologie des Sportes. In *Geschichte des Sportes aller Volker und Zeiten,* ed. G.A.E. Bogeng. Leipzig, Deutschland.

Wheaton, Belinda. 1997. "Covert Ethnography and the Ethics of Research." In *Ethics, Sport and Literature: Crises and Critiques,* ed. Tomlinson and Fleming. Aachen: Meyer and Meyer Verlag.

Whiting, R. 1976. *Chrysanthemum and the Bat: Baseball Samurai Style.* New York: Dodd, Mead.

Whiting, R. 1989. *You Gotta Have Wa.* New York: MacMillan.

Womack, Mari. 1992. "Why Athletes Need Ritual: A Study of Magic Among Professional Athletes." In *Sport and Religion,* ed. S. Hoffman. Champaign, IL: Human Kinetics.

Index

Italicized page numbers refer to photographs. Numbers followed by "n" indicate endnotes.

About the Author

The foremost authority in the field of sport and culture, Robert R. Sands, PhD, has published extensively on sport and culture. Sands, no stranger to participant-observation fieldwork, authored *Instant Acceleration: Living in the Fast Lane* and *Gutcheck! An Anthropologist's Wild Ride Into the Heart of College Football.* He also authored the first-ever primer on sport and culture, *Sport and Culture: At Play in the Fields of Anthropology,* and edited a first-ever volume on anthropology of sport, *Anthropology, Sport and Culture.*

Sands' unique hands-on participant-observation method of research not only produces an insider's perspective but also allows Sands to experience the same cultural experiences as those he is studying. He has studied African-American and Caucasian collegiate basketball players, African-American collegiate sprinters, and junior-college football teams. He is currently involved in participant-observation ethnography of the Southern California surfing culture.

Sands earned his doctorate in anthropology from the University of Illinois. He is currently conservation manager under contract to the Air Force at Edwards AFB, California.

*You'll find
other outstanding
sociology of sport resources at*

www.humankinetics.com

In the U.S. call

1-800-747-4457

Australia 08 8277 1555
Canada 1-800-465-7301
Europe .... +44 (0) 113 278 1708
New Zealand 09-523-3462

HUMAN KINETICS
The Information Leader in Physical Activity
P.O. Box 5076 • Champaign, IL 61825-5076 USA